Tying and Fishing
the
West's Best Dry Flies

By
Bob Wilson and Richard Parks

Photographs by R. Valentine Atkinson

Frank Amato Publications
P.O. Box 02112 Portland, Oregon 97202

ABOUT THE AUTHORS

BOB Wilson was an assemblyman for five years before being elected to the California State Senate for the 39th District in San Diego County. He is currently the Chairman of the Select Committee on Fish and Game Wildlife in the California State Senate. Bob received his B. S. degree in 1965 from California State Polytechnic University, San Luis Obispo, California. His J. D. degree followed in 1968 from the University of San Diego. Bob is also a practicing attorney. He has been an avid fly fisherman for over 20 years and has fished the Rivers Test and Itchen in England and most of the blue ribbon streams in the United States. Bob is currently a member of Cal-Trout, San Diego Fly Fishers, Trout Unlimited, F. F. F. and Gardiner Montana Fly Fishers.

RICHARD Parks is the manager of the Parks' Fly Shop in Gardiner, Montana. He has been a professional fly tier for over 20 years, starting to tie professionally at the age of 12. He has also been a river guide for 15 years. Richard received his B. A. degree from Montana State University. The Parks family has operated a quality fly tying shop in Gardiner, Montana, since 1953. And Richard has tested their products extensively throughout the West. Richard is a member of F. F. F., Trout Unlimited, and the Gardiner Montana Fly Fishers.

PHOTOGRAPHER, R. Valentine Atkinson, graduated from Columbus College of Art and Design, Columbus, Ohio, in 1969. After moving to the Bay Area and working for various advertising agencies and ABC television, he started free lancing in photography in San Francisco five years ago. He is affiliated with several diverse groups in the world of art, conservation, and fishing. Mr. Atkinson is a board member of San Francisco Camerawork, a non-profit organization dedicated to exhibiting fine photography, California Trout, and the Nature Conservancy.

All photographs in this book were taken in sequence with a 55 mm Nikor Macro lens, Plus-X film and natural light.

Caught in their respective tasks are Bob Wilson (left) writer and adviser, R. Valentine Atkinson (center) photographer, and Richard Parks (right) writer and fly tier.

Contents

Dedication

TO my late father, Merton Parks, who originated some of the patterns in this book and who was recognized as one of the West's finest dry fly fishermen.

Richard Parks

TO my parents, Jewell and Helen Wilson and to my brother, Wayne Wilson, who taught me to love trout fishing.

Bob Wilson

AND to all fishermen who release their fish unharmed.

Foreword

IN 1952 I was looking for retail shop accounts to get our wholesale tackle business off the ground, and Richard's late father, Merton Parks, was looking for a place to open a quality fly shop. Together, we found Gardiner to be a suitable location. Merton was an outstanding sportsman, a fine fisherman, and an excellent fly tier who quickly became a good friend as well.

Often I am asked to write forewords for books, and I usually turn them down. However, when Richard asked me to write the foreword for his and Bob's book, I said yes. I knew that Richard had literally grown up in the sport and knew the subject thoroughly. I had never had the opportunity to meet Bob except by reputation, but what I knew of him was good. My confidence was justified by the book, which is excellent.

To begin with, they approached quality fishing shops throughout the West. Here in my shop we are always receiving inquiries about what would be good to use in streams hundreds of miles away. The index of fly dressings which have been recommended by these shops serves as a badly needed comprehensive guide to just that sort of information, both for the flies themselves and for the shops which know their local waters intimately.

The West's many fast streams are often best approached with attractor patterns. Many of these streams are also very large, a factor which intimidates many fishermen used to smaller waters. In my days of fishing with Merton I could see that he had learned how, by expert reading, to cut even the largest river down to a manageable size. The basic principles of reading water are clearly set out, to enable the reader to put one of the carefully selected and proven attractor patterns in front of a fish.

Dry fly fishing and mayflies are nearly, if not quite, synonymous. The larger western rivers with their mixed hatches of mays, stones, and caddisflies are backed up by numerous spring creeks such as our own Armstrong and Nelson Creeks. Bob and Richard have selected a broad range of mayfly patterns which will serve any need. The heavily dressed impressionistic patterns are intended for the rough water streams where trout are not usually selective, while other patterns are aimed at those selective fish.

Caddisfly imitations are the current fad, but I think that they have selected the ones which will have enduring value. Stoneflies and terrestrials are another matter. Richard's father designed one of the best stonefly imitations, a pattern which has stood up to years of experience. Here again, they have selected the most generally useful patterns to tie.

Over the years I have found that there are a great many strongly held opinions on how to dress flies. I do not completely agree with Bob and Richard on certain aspects of their tying style. I prefer having both dry fly hackles facing dull side forward, and I have found hair tails to be satisfactory on all of my dries. With that said, between the excellent photography and the careful, detailed instructions, this is one of the best introductory manuals to dry fly tying available. The techniques section deals with major problem areas many tiers find very difficult. The result is a book which teaches how to tie virtually any type of dry fly.

Tying and Fishing the West's Best Dry Flies is a book which every fisherman with any ambition to fish the West should have. I believe it will prove to be a valuable addition to any fisherman's library.

Dan Bailey

Acknowledgements

W E wish to express our gratitude to each of the following persons whose generous help made this book possible.

Dan Bailey: The Dean of Western Dry Fly Fishermen, for his review of our manuscript, his encouragement and his willingness to write the foreword.

Dr. Ron Cordes: Author and Western Editor of Fly Fisherman Magazine for his helpful suggestions and his insight into the behavior of a trout.

Bob Quigley: Expert fly fisherman, fly tier, guide and owner of the Fall River Fly Shop at Rick's Lodge, Fall River, California, for his exhaustive review of the manuscript and helpful suggestions.

Richard May: President of CAL-TROUT and one who has done more to promote quality trout fishing in California than anyone we know, for his suggestions, criticisms and encouragement.

Dr. Tim Bywater: Professor of English and unofficially Professor of Fly Fishing, for spending countless hours helping to make our text read clearly.

Michael Fong: Author and one of the true masters on the dry fly for reviewing our manuscript and giving us some of his insights on fishing the dry fly.

Dr. Don Childress: Dentist and expert fly fisherman, for his advice and observations on the ways of a trout.

Ted Fay: Fly fishing guide in Dunsmuir, California, innovative fly tier and expert on the wet fly, for his advice, help and insights.

Bill Kiene: Owner of Fly Fishing Unlimited, Sacramento, California, for his insight into the mechanics of fly fishing.

Dick Kiene: Fly fisherman, artist and eternal seeker of rainbow, for his advice and encouragement.

Walton Powell: Expert rod builder and fly fisherman, for relating to us the history of the Buzz Hackle Fly and sending us samples of how the Buzz Hackle should be tied.

Ellen Parks and Sharman Wilson: For deciphering our handwriting, typing the manuscript, spending many hours writing to Western Fly Fishing Shops asking for their favorite patterns, and most of all for creating order out of chaos.

And finally to all of the owners of Western Fly Fishing Shops that sent us a listing of their favorite dry fly patterns for inclusion in this book. Without their help this book would not have been possible.

Introduction

THIS is not a book of fishing stories, but rather a book that sets forth, hopefully in a succinct manner without fanfare, practical tips on how to catch fish so that you will have your own fish stories to tell. Secondly, and just as important, this is a book of step-by-step fly tying instructions intended to teach the beginner as well as the experienced tier to tie flies of professional quality.

In order to determine the West's best dry flies, we wrote to almost every fly shop in the western United States asking for their five favorite dry flies. The names and addresses of those shops that responded, along with their fly selections, are listed in the back of this book. Most of these selections are favorite dry flies for each shop's particular geographical area and could be used as a guide when fishing these areas. The dressing for each pattern is either listed in the step-by-step fly tying section of the book or in the dressing section at the end of the book. In all, over 130 dry fly dressings are given. Those fly patterns that proved to be the most popular are tied in the book, using step-by-step instructions along with photographs of each step.

The sections in this book dealing with fly tying, tools and materials, and fly tying techniques, were written by Richard Parks. Those chapters or sections dealing with mayfly, caddisfly, stonefly, terrestrials, attractor imitations, and conservation were written by Bob Wilson. The section on reading the water represents the thoughts of both authors.

Chapter I

Tools and Materials

THE basic tools of fly casting are the rod, reel, and line. These must be matched in a balanced outfit. While this comprises the minimum equipment to catch a fish on fly tackle, you will almost certainly find other accessories desirable. Some of these accessories make the process of fly fishing more efficient or comfortable and some expand the sport into other areas. Many fly fishermen find tying their own flies a fascinating addition to the sport, thereby generating additional tool and material requirements.

There are nearly as many conflicting opinions on the selection of rods, reels, and lines as there are anglers. We have seen people attempting to fly fish with equipment ranging in price from $15.00 to $1,000.00 and doing equally well. This is by no means to say that equipment is not important – just that there are other factors that are just as important. Most of this book is about those factors. The fact remains that most people will get more satisfaction from fly fishing or any other activity with equipment that functions properly.

The physical basis of fly casting is straight forward. A lever, the rod, is used to accelerate a projectile, the line. The line is stored on a rotating drum, the reel. The mechanical objective is to deliver a nearly weightless object with a good deal of air resistance, the fly, to a distant point. In the direct sense you do this in order to catch a fish. The ultimate justification, however, is not the catching of fish, but rather the pleasure derived by doing so.

RODS: In general, you get what you pay for. It is still possible to outfit a fisherman for less than $25.00 and give him a reasonable chance to catch a fish. However, the first few additional dollars spent on a fly outfit buys the greatest increment in quality. Glass rods are available for under $10.00, but don't buy them unless you absolutely must. Several manufacturers produce useful rods in the $15.00 to $30.00 price range. One piece of advice which applies throughout this discussion is to buy your equipment from a fly fishing specialty shop. The operator of such a store fishes with what he sells, ties flies in many cases, and will in general be your best source of information. He is likely to tell you if a given rod or other item suits your needs at a fair price.

Between $30.00 and $50.00 there is a gap in the quality gained by spending additional dollars. A $40.00 rod is sometimes a bargain $50.00 rod, but more often it is a $20.00 rod with a fancy paint job. Fenwick glass rods are the standard rods in the $50.00 bracket. They are the least expensive rods that I would consider for myself.

Above $50.00 the quality of glass rods takes a quantum leap over the lower categories. There are many excellent rods in this bracket, including the "name" manufacturers such as Orvis, Scientific Anglers, and Winston. Smaller manufacturers such as Powell and Claudio also make very fine glass rods. Conventional glass rods reach the limits of their functional improvement at about $100.00. The higher price charged for the famous maker's name and superior rod cosmetics may be sufficiently justified in your eyes, but be sure you understand this before making the purchase.

Graphite provides the next increment in rod quality. The light weight and high modulus (stiffness) of graphite combine to make it the best contemporary rod material for distance casting. The greater stiffness of graphite means that more of the casting energy is transferred to the line. This energy is translated into casting range. Unfortunately the greater stiffness also means that short lines do not load the rod. The resulting loss of casting efficiency and accuracy at short ranges is the major drawback with graphite. The same qualities of lightness and stiffness make it possible to achieve a combination heretofore impossible — the long (nine feet and up), light rod carrying a light (five weight or under) line.

It is difficult to make generalizations about prices of graphite rods, since the field is still new and subject to rapid changes of quality and price. The least expensive graphite rod I would consider is the Powell. These rods are retailing at about $90.00 and are an excellent value. Again, the advice of your professional specialty shop operator can help you sort the wheat from the chaff. As always, the major manufacturers, Fenwick and Cortland for example, all have excellent rods. The prices vary a great deal with the specifications and manufacturer.

Cane rods, once the standard, have become status symbols. We like our cane rods but, to be candid, one generally pays a lot of money for cane that cannot be justified by objective criteria. The top manufacturers of cane are selling their rods for $300.00 to $400.00. It is improbable that a new top quality cane rod will be available for less. I fish dry flies with cane as a matter of personal enjoyment, but my graphite and good quality glass rods are excellent performers.

The balance between stiffness (modulus) and the damping qualities of bamboo gives it the ability to cast accurately at varying, relatively short ranges. This is terribly important because most effective dry fly fishing is done between 15 and 30 feet. Even the best of glass rods have rebounding vibrations while the line is still airborne after the forward cast. The improvement of damping qualities (the reduction of vibration) is one of the things that you pay for in a good glass rod. Stiffness translates as power for the distance cast. Graphite is supreme in this respect. Of course at short ranges power is not the prime requirement.

When all is said and done, the reason I prefer bamboo is just because I like it. That is the ultimate justification.

Before going on to talk about rod specifications, I would like to say a little about building your own rod. Contrary to popular belief, you still get just about what you pay for. A glass blank and components costing about $25.00 will produce a rod that would sell commercially for about $40.00 to $50.00. The project is often worth doing just for your own satisfaction, but do not kid yourself into believing that you are saving a lot of money. At the moment good graphite blanks cost about $60.00 and compatible hardware will add $10.00 to $15.00 to the cost. This is a better savings, but the finished product carries none of the guarantees that the manufacturer places on his own equipment.

The rod that is best for you will vary depending on the type of fishing you do. Few serious fly fishermen have been able to restrict themselves to only one rod. This discussion is oriented toward western dry fly fishing and my recommendation reflects my own prejudices as much as anything else. Regardless of the price range you ultimately select, look for a rod of 8 feet to 8½ feet for a 6 or 7 weight line. Such a rod enables you to realistically fish dry flies, nymphs, and large streamers.

I do not care much for shorter rods because they require more work and casting timing is more critical to get the same results. Remember that the rod is a lever. A longer lever has a greater mechanical advantage. As the rod gets shorter the timing of each casting stroke becomes progressively more critical. This is a problem for an experienced angler. Those less experienced should give themselves every break by sticking to longer, more forgiving rods. Longer rods provide an additional advantage after the cast is completed. A critical problem in dry fly fishing is drag. The long rod allows you to avoid drag by keeping less line on the water.

LINES: Dry fly fishing requires floating lines. Modern synthetic fly lines are very much superior to lines made as little as ten years ago. The top lines sell for around $17.00 to $20.00. Second rate lines can be secured for $8.00 to $15.00. The principal tradeoff made for price is durability. The following tradeoffs sacrifice some of the floating and casting characteristics. Don't buy an inexpensive line unless you have no choice.

Synthetic materials have made it possible to offer a bewildering array of lines. The American Fishing Tackle Manufacturers Association has established a uniform nomenclature which is used to describe all fly lines. This nomenclature uses a three-part description to identify all lines. The first part is a pair of letters which describes the type of taper. All level lines are designated with the single letter "L," but do not bother with them. These letters, "DT," "WF" or "ST" designate respectively a "double taper," a "weight forward" and a "single, or shooting, taper" line.

The second part of the nomenclature is a number. This is an index number giving the weight of the first 30 feet of the line. Most rods will be keyed to a line weight that works best with them. This eliminates the need for the average fisherman to know exactly what his line weighs. If you have a rod which does not have this number on it, usually included with the manufacturer's name and the model number near the butt of the rod, visit your local fly shop to clear up the matter.

Most rods will work with a line one size larger or smaller than optimum. The length of line which you normally carry in the air will affect the size line which works best, as will the distance that you are routinely trying to reach. More than 30 feet of line in the air adds weight beyond the rod tip, thus allowing a lighter line to load the rod with the optimum weight. Conversely, short casts such as those usually required on small rough water mean less line in the air. A heavier line is then required to reach the design weight.

The third part of the nomenclature is formed from more letters. "F" means that the line floats, "S" means it sinks. "F/S" means that part of the line floats, but the forward part sinks. This last designation is usually accompanied by a manufacturer's description indicating how much of the line sinks. "Sink-tip" indicates that only the first ten feet of the line sinks. "Sink-belly" usually means that the first 30 feet of the line sinks.

It is probable that the debate as to the relative merits of weight forward versus double taper lines will never be settled. The great advantage of weight forward lines is their superiority for long casting. An advantage of the double taper line is its ability to turn over the leader and fly on short casts, a feature particularly important to the dry fly fisherman. In dry fly fishing long casts are frequently counter productive. With few exceptions, most dry fly fishing is done at ranges of less than 30 feet.

Frequently cited as a disadvantage of the double taper is the space it takes up on the reel. The easy solution to this problem also saves money. I cut my double taper lines at their midpoint, storing the unused half of the lines in a closet. The remaining lines are brand new when they are called to action. Then I prepare the reel with an ample supply of backing, against the chance of hooking a really large fish.

Almost anything can be used for backing which is nothing but extra line in reserve, "backing" the regular line. I find dacron trolling line works well for me. Amnesia and other monofilament materials can be used as backing, but they are really intended for use as the running line behind a shooting head. They should never be attached directly to the spool of the reel without a cushion of some other backing, since they can shrink, crushing the center of the reel.

REELS: The reel is described as nothing but a spool to hold line. In practice, your reel can literally make or break your affair with a large fish. There are three basic types of fly reels — automatics, multipliers, and single actions. Avoid the automatics, as they are heavy and fragile. Multipliers are geared reels. These have their uses, but get some expert advice from your local specialist before selecting one. All of my reels are sturdy, single action reels.

As with rods, there is a wide variety of price and quality available in fly reels. Do not spend less than $12.00 for a reel. Less expensive reels have inferior or non-existent drags and poor engineering standards. Inexpensive reels are usually made without extra spools and in only one size. The Pfleuger "1535" may be the best buy in an inexpensive reel. Berkley's "556" makes an excellent reel in the $20.00 to $25.00 class. These reels can generally be changed to wind with either hand and extra spools are generally available. Individual reels of the same manufacturer and model may vary a good deal. Reject any reel on which the spool rubs against the rim of the frame. This invariably places severe strains on your leader, causing it to break.

The better engineered reels are all in the $40.00 to $70.00 class. Unfortunately, few of them have a really adequate drag, but some do have an outside rim which can be palmed for additional control. The Hardy Perfect, Scientific Angler and Orvis CFO reels come to mind. The best built fly reels are $100.00 to $200.00, but these reels are all oriented toward saltwater or heavy streamer fishing. In general they are too heavy for dry fly fishing. What may prove to be an excellent compromise between weight and a really good drag has just come to my attention. The "1781" and "156" Abu Cardinals marketed by Zebco have a good disc drag system but weigh only a little more than similarly sized conventional reels.

Whatever the price range you select, get a reel large enough to hold the line you are using plus at least 20 yards of braided Dacron backing without overfilling the spool. If you are using half of a double taper, then you should have a minimum of 50 yards of backing. You won't need it often, but when you do need it you will want it very badly.

Balancing an outfit is not as difficult as it is sometimes made out to be. Select the rod and line together and be sure that the reel has sufficient capacity for the line. Try testing with a friend's gear whenever possible before making a major purchase. Rods vary in weight from under two ounces to well over six ounces. Reels, without lines, weigh from two ounces to nearly a pound. Mismatching the extremes is not a good idea. A poorly balanced rod/reel system tires the fisherman's casting arm. Ideally, the rod with reel and line mounted should balance at the front of the handle. A need for large line capacity or heavy drag usually means having to accept a somewhat heavier reel than optimum. A wide range of reel weights will function on any given rod. Variations from the theoretical ideal do not become critical until you approach the extremes.

LEADERS: More confusion arises over leaders than any other part of the casting system. Widely expounded and mutually contradictory theories of leader design account for a good part of the trouble. Wildly varying fishing conditions, each with its own requirements, accounts for some of the confusion. An inherently confusing nomenclature accounts for most of the rest.

The theory that leaders should have soft butts to continue the diameter and flex of the line is a fundamentally mistaken concept. Both Bob Wilson and I have tried such systems. We have found them incapable of turning a fly over under any but the best of conditions. We recommend splicing an 18-inch butt of hard monofilament, at least 0.020 inch in diameter, to your line before tying on a standard tapered leader.

Differing conditions require differing leaders. Broken water, where short casts are the rule, and windy conditions during which turn over becomes difficult demand short leaders. Under these conditions I recommend 7½ foot leaders. Flat water or selective fish, usually occurring together, require longer leaders such as a 9 footer. My leader length, including the 18 inch butt section, generally ranges from 8 feet to 11½ feet. Only the most extreme conditions warrant longer leaders. Most casting situations are at ranges under 30 feet. Casting nothing but a leader is difficult to manage.

The nomenclature used to describe leaders and leader materials confuses many. The basic problem is that monofilament is described by three different systems based on two partially independent variables. The labels of most leader materials usually describe the contents in terms of test strength in pounds or, increasingly, in kilograms; in terms of diameter as ten-thousands of an inch; and in terms of "X" number, which is also an expression of diameter. The test strength system tells us how strong a material is, but gives no clue to its diameter. The diameter systems don't tell us anything about the strength. Since strength-to-diameter ratios vary greatly with the specific material, there is no set way to convert one to the other.

The diameter of a material is more important to the fly fisherman than absolute strength. Unfortunately manufacturers are not always able to completely control the diameter of their materials. Leaders often vary from the stated diameter. Your specialty store usually has a micrometer to enable you to deal with true diameters.

If you are explicit in explaining to your dealer what sort of fishing you expect to be doing, he will recommend the leaders and leader material best suited for you. Do not try to save money on the leader. Do not stray very far from the leader-fly sizes recommended on the table. A leader too large for the work produces a sloppy, splashy delivery. A leader too small for the work fails to straighten out, leaving the fly in the middle of a rat's nest.

LEADER SIZE TABLE

Size Fly	"X Number	Diameter in Thousandths of an Inch
No. 6 and larger	0X	0.011 and up
No. 8	1X	0.010
No. 10	2X	0.009
No. 12	3X	0.008
No. 14 and No. 16	4X	0.007
No. 18	5X	0.006
No. 18	6X	0.005
No. 20 and No. 22	7X	0.004
No. 24 and smaller	8X	0.003

ACCESSORIES: We have found it impossible to fish without getting in the water. This requires either a willingness to get wet and cold or the purchase of waders. Waders are of two types – stocking foot and boot foot. Stocking foot waders require wading shoes. Without doubt, the best stocking foot wader is the Seal-Dry. Converse's imported felt sole wader may be the most effective of the boot-foot waders. We have to say that we are not terribly pleased with the present wader situation, where quality seems to be mostly bad and worse. Do not under any circumstances spend less than about $30.00 for wading gear. Take your dealer's advice on what to purchase. Purchase a patching kit at the same time you buy waders. The melting stick type patch is strictly an emergency measure which cannot effect a permanent repair. The best permanent kit will depend on the wader materials. Your dealer will be able to advise you on this and other accessory purchases.

The angler's usual collection of fly boxes, small tools and supplies quickly overflows pants and shirt pockets. Nothing is as satisfactory for organizing this gear as a vest. Vests of satisfactory quality run from $19.00 to nearly $100.00. The principal variable in price is the number of pockets provided.

FLY TYING TOOLS: I suspect more people have been turned away from fly tying by poor tools than any other single cause. Most fly tying kits are not worth the money spent on them because they generally present inadequate tools and poorly assorted materials. Many beginning tiers also find themselves burdened with gadgets at the expense of essential items.

Vise: Some people tie flies without a vise at all. Believe me, this is the hard way to do it, but I would rather work without a vise than with a poor one. The vise I use is the Thompson Model "A." Presently selling for about $23.00, this vise features adjustable jaws and height relative to the table top. It also rotates about its vertical axis, which allows it to be used by either a left or right handed person. Less expensive vises work satisfactorily but they are not as durable. The jaws themselves eventually fatigue and break. Thompson provides replacement jaw kits which are not available for other vises.

The expensive semi-custom vises are beautiful to behold but not very cost-effective. The satisfaction attained by having the best of something may justify its purchase. A "midge" vise is worth considering if you expect to tie large numbers of tiny flies. The Croydon is an excellent little hand-held vise for streamside tying.

Scissors: You must get a quality pair of scissors. Scissors should have large enough finger holes to handle easily. If possible, try them on before you buy to make sure your fingers comfortably fit the handle. At the same time they must have the fine points which enable you to get them into the close work required by small flies. These scissors generally run about $5.00 per pair. I prefer the straight bladed scissor for myself, but would not argue against the curved scissor.

Bobbin: The bobbin is another tool that some people do without, but it certainly simplifies the tying process. A bobbin is essentially nothing but a device to hold the spool of tying thread under tension. I use the Matarelli style bobbin which costs under $5.00. There are several bobbins of this type on the market and any of them except the cheapest are usable. These bobbins all accept the standard size spools of thread. I would avoid a bobbin that required a special spool, since that ordinarily requires respooling your thread. The bobbins with flared tubes such as the Creative Sports bobbin can be used with thread but are particularly useful for bulky materials like floss or tinsel thread.

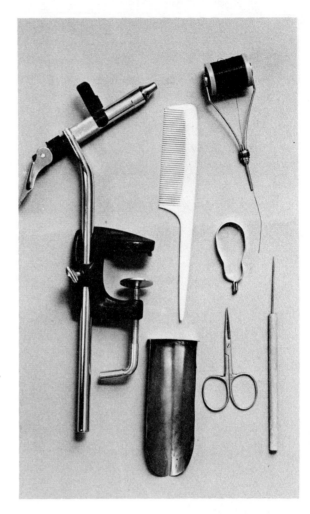

Hackle Pliers: Hackle pliers provide a firm grip on the point of a hackle, a most useful feature especially when dealing with small flies. I use the Thompson "midget" pliers, but any plier with narrow jaws will work. The wide jaw pliers do not allow you to get close enough to the work. Since the unadorned hard metal edges of most pliers cut the stems of the feathers, the pliers need to be modified by padding them with something like the soft plastic tubing used as model airplane fuel line. Hackle pliers also serve admirably as a third hand, temporarily securing materials such as a broken thread. Hackle pliers generally cost $1.00 to $2.00.

Bodkin: A bodkin is nothing but a needle on a stick. The standard dissecting needle available from campus stores makes an excellent bodkin for about $0.20. The bodkin acts as an applicator for lacquer and cement. It also serves as a dubbing tool and to maintain loop tension on the hand thrown whip finish. The multitude of uses to which it can be put makes it a hard tool to do without. I have seen these things priced as high as $2.00 but none of them will do anything that can't be done with the dissecting needle.

Hair Stacker: The hair stacker simplifies operations with hair to such a degree that I consider it an essential tool. There are two types — the open trough stacker and the closed cartridge tube stacker. I prefer the open stacker because it facilitates working with the hair. They cost $1.00 to $2.00. The closed tube style of stacker costs much more and, because it is closed, limits your access to the hair during the stacking process. The original hair stacker was made by taking tin snips to a small tobacco tin. You can do the same but the small savings realized is not worth the effort.

Supplementary Tools: A number of specialty tools supplement the basic kit. These devices either perform a special limited task or tasks which can be performed without a tool.

Whip Finisher: Most fly tiers use a whip finish tool. I believe the hand thrown whip finish to be superior. The major problem is that the whip finisher will not work in certain situations, but half-hitches, which require no tool but the bodkin, can be used instead.

Comb: A regular comb with a handle helps a great deal in working hair. A few strokes with the comb removes most of the underfur from a hair bundle. It is not, however, a complete answer. The tines on even a fine comb are far enough apart to pass quite a lot of objectionable material.

Materials Clip: The materials clip holds long strands of material out of the way of the work. It is seldom of much use to the dry fly tier, but is nearly indispensable to the streamer tier. There are two general types. One looks like a coil spring and the other like a leaf spring. I have had better success with the latter.

Hackle Guards and Gauges: Hackle guards and gauges fall into the gadget category. Your fingers make a better and cheaper hackle guard. Hackle gauges are of some use to the beginner until he picks up the experience of judging hackle sizes.

Half Hitch Tool: The half hitch tool is another gadget item. Its redundancy with the whip finisher makes it pretty useless. Like with the whip finisher, there are situations when a half hitch tool cannot be used.

Mini-Blender: The mini-blender eases preparation of the basic fur ball for dubbed bodies. Hand blending of any sizeable amount of dubbing fur quickly demonstrates the justification for meeting the hefty $20.00 to $30.00 purchase price.

FLY TYING MATERIALS: The following discussion is limited to the major materials for dressing dry flies. The accumulation of tying materials threatens to become a hobby in itself. Eric Leiser's *Fly Tying Materials* thoroughly discusses the acquisition, storage and application of all types of tying materials. I recommend constant vigilance whenever you enter a store selling materials. If you find anything extraordinary that you expect to use, buy it. It may never be so easy to find again. Make material purchases from someone who actually ties flies. You will find that such a person better understands what you are trying to do.

Hooks: There is no substitute for the right hook. The tying instructions for each fly list the hook and sizes recommended for that fly. You will note that all hooks are either the standard shank fine wire hook, Mustad 94840, the 2X long shank hook, Mustad 9671, or the short shank fine wire hook, Mustad 94838. Very fine wire hooks are not recommended; they are too easy to bend or break. The reduction in weight is not an adequate compensation.

All of these hooks are forged, turned-down eye hooks. We would recommend that you use a ringed eye hook on flies size 22 and smaller. In my experience it seldom works well to use a tiny fly for its own sake. Use as large a hook as the situation created by the natural allows. The improvement in hooking and holding usually compensates for any reduction in the number of strikes.

Thread: The standard tying thread these days is Danville's mono-cord. These threads can be purchased from most materials houses in a range of sizes and colors. We recommend size "A" mono-cord only for flies size 10 and larger. We use 3/0 mono-cord on our flies in sizes 12 through 16, and 6/0 pre-waxed thread on smaller hooks. The dressing instructions included with each fly pattern specifies the thread required.

Head Cement and Adhesives: Head cements are usually lacquer, which is just paint. It is adequate for most purposes, but it is not a glue. I have had excellent results from Duco Cement, a clear acetate cement with a fairly short setting time. Most head cements can be thinned with the acetone used to thin the Duco, but you should be sure to have a thinner for the head cement. I don't care for wax in dubbing fur bodies. I use spar varnish instead.

Acquire a can of Grumbacher "Tuffilm" spray to treat all turkey and other wing quills being used for rolled wings. Examples of flies requiring this technique are the Grasshopper and King's River Caddis.

Tail Materials: Numerous materials are used in the tails of flies and there is a great deal of interchangeability between them. The classic dry fly patterns rely on hackle fiber tails. The hackles selected for this should come from the sides of the neck. It is here that the stiff, long barbuled feathers ideal for this purpose are found. Tails of any useful color are readily achieved through the magic of the dye pot. I do not approve of the wholesale substitution of hair for hackle fiber tails. Both color tones and durability are sacrificed. Hackle stems stripped of their barbules are sometimes used as tails, but dyed monofilament produces the same effect with less effort. Golden pheasant tippet makes an excellent tail material.

In their original applications, hair tails make excellent sense. Bucktail provides most of the tail fibers I use. The natural reddish brown color of the tail's top side is just right for many flies, while the white side can be dyed to any color. The body hair of moose, elk and deer are also useful as tail materials.

Body Materials: An enormous variety of materials have been used to make fly bodies. Some are very straight forward and can be purchased in virtually any shop selling materials. Others have only limited uses and availability.

Chenille is an excellent wet fly body material. Its bulk and tendency to absorb water, however, make it something to be avoided in dry fly applications.

Tinsel is most often used in conjunction with other body materials. On dry flies its usual application is as a rib or underbody. It is the only material that can be employed for the purpose of imparting a metallic sheen to the fly. Flat mylar tinsel has a silver and a gold side so that it can be used for either color on the body. The new tinsel thread put out by Creative Sports is an excellent material. It may replace oval tinsel wherever strength is required, particularly since it is available in several colors.

A few flies, notably the Bunyon Bug, a salmon fly imitation, use the stem of a wing quill to form the body. These make virtually unsinkable flies but I have not been impressed with their effectiveness as imitations.

A more commonly used material is floss. Its ease of handling makes it a very popular body material. It is generally employed with a rib of tinsel or palmer hackle when it is the major body material. The bright red color segment on flies like the Royal Wulff is floss. Most flosses are rayon but an acetate based floss can be substituted. Painting floss with acetone after the fly is completed causes the fibers to melt together to make a hard shell.

Various types of plumage are used as body materials. The most familiar are peacock and ostrich herl. Peacock is uniquely irridescent and attractive to fish. The eye of the peacock, when the strands are stripped of their flue, provides the best quill body material. Ostrich herl can be dyed to meet almost any color requirement. The expense of ostrich herl reduces its attractiveness for applications where it is not required. Hackle feathers are also used as a body material. When used in the body of a fly, hackle is described as "Palmer style" hackle. The BiVisible patterns employ a Palmer hackle, while Joe's Hopper and Salmon Fly utilize a clipped Palmer tied as a rib over another body material. Some effective patterns call for a quill body made by stripping all the barbules from a hackle stem. The stripped hackle stem, when wound onto the hook, produces a more finely segmented body than can be achieved with the peacock quill. You may achieve a wide variety of body color tones by the choice of the colors exhibited by the thread underbody and the original hackle stem.

Bodies made of hair generally are produced by using one of two techniques. The body hair of deer, elk, caribou, or any hollow hair, may be spun and clipped to form the body of a fly such as the Irresistible. These hairs may be dyed to achieve the desired color tones. The second technique is to use a hank of hair parallel to the hook as a body segment. Many extended body Mayfly patterns also utilize hair this way. Any of these hairs may be substituted for each other, but each fly ties best with a particular hair. There is a wide variation in the coarseness and color tones of hair, even from the same animal, that affects the eventual product. Hair of large outside diameter, coarseness, that is also hollow, such as the base hair from a bucktail and body hair sections from elk, deer and caribou, make the best hair to spin for clipped hair bodies.

Many yarns are adaptable to fly tying. Select orlon, acrylic, or other synthetic yarns. They do not soak water as badly as wool yarns. Most synthetic yarns are very strong. The strength of the material is directly related to the fiber length. These materials usually have long fibers.

The soft yarn called "spun fur" makes a very good looking body. This material, usually spun from the Angora rabbit, exhibits the translucent qualities of other natural furs. Unlike most yarns, however, it is composed of fairly short fibers. It is weaker and more likely to break while you are tying with it.

A nylon-acrylic blended yarn marketed under names such as "Dazzle" or "Sparkle Yarn" makes excellent caddis bodies. A full range of colors can usually be found in yarn shops as well as materials houses. Another group of yarns which have become very popular of late is the polypropalene yarns. Their biggest advantage to the dry fly tier is their positive buoyancy. The uniformity and solid outline produced by these materials, however, does not simulate well the translucent variations of natural insects. Yarns are ordinarily available in a wide range of colors which satisfy most color requirements.

Most dry fly bodies requiring fur are either gray or cream. The standard gray fur is the common muskrat, while cream is provided by the fitch, a small animal similar to a weasel. The underfur on the pelt is the most useful material for dubbing. The color of the stiff outer hairs, called "guard hairs," is irrelevant, since these will be discarded anyway. Rabbit or any other gray underfur of fine texture can be substituted for muskrat, and fitch can be replaced by the cream belly fur of the fox and several other beasts. Beaver and otter provide tan shades, while mink produces a dark color.

Synthetic dubbing materials, particularly polypropalene, may be substituted for any of the natural furs. When dubbed, poly materials regain the translucence they lose as a yarn. The spun furs may be picked apart and blended with natural furs, or with each other, to achieve new color tones, matching some particular natural.

Wing Materials: The variety of wing materials rivals that of body materials. The great bulk of flies use hair or wings formed from hackle points, flank feathers, or wing quills.

Hair wings generally employ bucktail, calf tail, deer body or elk body hair. Any of these materials can be dyed to achieve the required color tones. The principal variables encountered in hairs are the degree of hollowness of the individual hairs, their outside diameters, and their color tones. The less hollow, finer hairs of the bucktail make the best wings. Select the finer body hairs for wings as well. Exceptions to this generalization are found in flies such as the Bucktail Caddis, on which the wing hairs should spray out like a fan.

Hackle point wings are characteristic of flies like the Adams. These wings are simply the tips of hackle feathers, usually grizzly. Other feathers can be employed to achieve differing effects. A similar wing is the fanwing, which uses the tiny breast feathers of ducks.

Many flies employ woodduck or mallard flank feathers to make the wing. Woodduck is expensive, but the barred tan tones can be simulated almost exactly with dyed mallard, which is generally available and much less costly. The natural dark barring on a gray background of the mallard feather also makes it an effective wing.

The wing feathers of ducks, geese, and turkeys are usually referred to as "quills" but should not be confused with the peacock or hackle stem quill body. Various color effects can be readily achieved by dyeing these feathers. Mottled turkey wing quills make the best grasshopper wings. Unfortunately the demand for turkeys with more white meat has resulted in breeding a white turkey that has lost the mottling in the wings. Body feathers from the common ringneck pheasant make an acceptable substitute for some applications.

Hackle Materials: The term "hackle" refers to those feathers which come from the neck and saddle of chickens. Saddle hackles are those feathers taken from the bird's back. Neck hackles come literally from the neck of the bird. Feathers to be used as dry fly hackle must come from roosters. The barbules of hen hackles are simply too soft to float a fly. The other meaning of the term "hackle" is the collar wound around the fly, a feather which creates a uniform spray of fibers at right angles to the hook. Hackles in this sense are usually hackle feathers, but they can be of hair as well. George Grant explains his theories of hair hackles in *The Art of Weaving Hair Hackles for Trout Flies*. This technique replaces ordinary feather hackle with hair hackle. The preparation time makes the hair hackle technique impractical for commercial tiers, but it should not deter the amateur.

The quality of hackle feathers varies tremendously. If possible, personally inspect all hackles you intend to purchase. Unfortunately no standard nomenclature exists to describe the colors

18

of hackle feathers. The hackle from the Plymouth Rock chicken is usually referred to as grizzly or barred rock though it is also called gray. Many chickens such as the Rhode Island Red have the hackles which are usually described as brown or dark ginger. Coachman brown usually refers to a very dark chocolate brown color. Ginger can mean anything from a light brown to cream. I generally take it to mean a natural light yellowish tan. Furnace is a natural brown feather with a dark, nearly black center. Badger is a cream feather with a black center. Blue dun or dun refers to a natural or dyed blue-gray color. There are numerous shades of dun hackles grading into cream on the light end and black on the dark end of the spectrum. I specify light dun when I mean a nearly cream hackle, and charcoal when I mean nearly black.

Securing brown hackle presents no difficulty, while grizzly is generally available but at a high price. Natural duns and blacks are much rarer, but fortunately these shades can easily and satis-factorily be achieved by dyeing other necks. Natural ginger is fairly rare, and the bleached necks used as a substitute never look quite right. Whites and creams are usually available, as are furnace and badger. Most flies specifying furnace or badger can be tied with brown or cream with equal results.

In shopping for hackle you should find that price is directly related to quality and scarcity. Most shops grade their hackles with the top grade going to necks or saddles which have more small feathers of excellent stiffness. Second grade necks usually have adequate feather quality but larger feathers. They are often the best compromise between price and quality. Grizzly, natural ginger, natural blacks and natural duns are the rarest and most expensive necks, while brown is common and relatively cheap.

The materials merchant who ties flies himself is your best source, as he can help you with substitutions, color selections and quality compromises. Most such houses carry a stock of all really necessary feathers. We do not recommend doing your own dyeing unless you expect to use large quantities of one color. Major materials houses do custom dyeing if your requirements are unusual.

Establishing a Tying Station: If you can appropriate a permanent space in which to do your tying it will save setup and cleanup time. The location must be reasonably protected from drafts, dogs, children and other household pets. A nearby electric outlet provides a place to plug in a lamp and the mini-blender. Carpeted areas should be avoided if possible to avoid potential dam-age to the rug. The person responsible for house cleaning will soundly curse the perverse ability of a fly tier to drop tiny hooks in the carpet.

A device called the Waste-troll reduces the spread of such garbage. It is a wire frame holding a plastic bag clamped under the vise. It catches the trimmings and, when used in combination with a trash container, prevents a good deal of friction with other members of the household. A certain

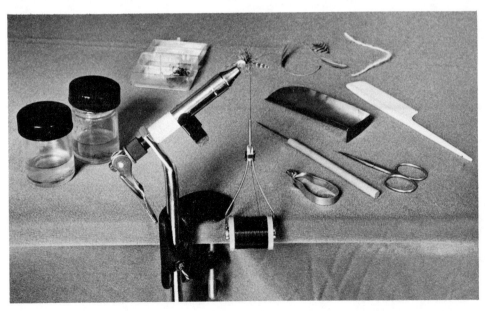

number of spills are inevitable. I wear an apron made from an old terry towel to clean my bodkin after each trip to the lacquer or glue bottle and as a first line of defense against spills.

A clear table space about two feet square is required. The edge of the table should extend enough to allow the vise to be clamped to it. Cover the surface with a disposable material to protect it from spills and the vise clamp. You should also provide yourself with a small flexible desk lamp. Working without one is a headache.

Material requires storage space in proximity to the tying station. A small-parts drawer easily accommodates hooks, thread, small tools, floss, tinsel, and other items of this sort. A few drawers or similar sized boxes will do for necks, large tools, hair and other bulky materials. For the storage of loose feathers buy a box of business sized envelopes. Label the envelopes as required; for example, "Blue dun neck hackle – dry No. 16." The box itself serves as a file to organize the envelopes and facilitate the retrieval of feathers as needed.

Secure one to three dozen banker's pins. Push these half-inch long straight pins through a piece of cardboard, forming rows, and turn the cardboard so the pinpoints are up. As you finish each fly place its eye over one of the pins in this "bed of nails." This eliminates any possibility of having the eye fouled with lacquer when you attempt to tie it to your leader late at night when the fish are rising.

Develop an arrangement for the tools, fly board, sorting tray and materials which satisfies you. I find that tools under my right hand are instantly available. Placing the lacquer and cement bottles on the left reduces the chance of spillage. Each tier will have to work out his own satisfactory arrangement.

Chapter II

Basic Fly Tying Techniques

THE biggest problem most tiers experience is materials control. The tendency is to use too much of everything, which results in a weak, poorly performing fly. Unfortunately, the only way I know to gain experience in judging materials is to tie often. Practice each step until you master it. If you are a beginning tier, buy a pack of single edge razor blades. Be ruthless in your self-critique and don't hesitate to use the razor blade to clean hooks. Watch other tiers whenver you can, questioning them when possible about their techniques.

There are a couple of questions of nomenclature to clear up before beginning. Throughout this discussion, "open turns" means winding the thread or material with a space between turns. "Close turns" means placing each new turn right next to the previous one. When I specify Duco, I mean Duco cement thinned with acetone. "Lacquer" or "cement" is ordinary head cement, and "varnish" is spar varnish. The instruction "to attach" means usually to use just enough turns of the thread to hold the materials in place. "To secure" means using close turns to firmly *bind* everything in place. Unless specifically stated otherwise, every turn of any material must be made with sufficient uniform pressure to create a tight, durable fly.

Fly Proportions

Throughout this discussion of basic techniques and the detailed instructions for the flies, I make references to fly proportions. The basic unit of measurement on a hook is the gape. The hook size, say size 12, simply designates this gape. All size 12 hooks have, in theory, the same gape. The overall size of the fly, however, also depends on the shank length. Since the gape is required for proper hooking, small flies generally achieve better results when tied on a short shank hook one size larger than the regular shank hook. As an example, the size 16 Quill Gordon on the short shank hook is about the same overall size as the size 18 on a regular hook. But a size 16 short shank hook holds hooked fish more securely.

Tails usually equal twice the gape of the hook on all flies. The shank length of a regular shank hook is also twice the gape. Any exceptions to this rule are noted in the tying instructions for dressing the fly. The tail is always secured to the hook at the point where the bend meets the shank of the hook.

The body also begins at this point. On regular shank hooks the body is as long as the gape is wide. On long and short shank hooks the body length is determined by the wing position. In any case, if the fly is a downwing fly like the Trude, the body ends at the wing position.

The wing position on regular shank hooks is determined by the mid-point between the eye of the fly and the point of the hook. The same rule works for long shank hooks. The hackle and wing require just as much space on the short shank as they do on the regular hook. The difference can be made up by shortening the body and moving the wing position back to the mid-point of the shank. Wings themselves equal the overall length of the hook, which in turn is just slightly more than twice the gape. Downwings are often exceptions to this rule.

Hackle size again relates to the hook gape. The standard proportion fixes the length of an individual hackle barbule at twice the gape dimension. Flies designated as variants, however, require hackle sized as if the hook were two sizes larger — that's why they are called *variants*. Any departures from this rule are noted in the instructions.

If these rules are followed, a space should remain at the front of the hook in which to tie materials off and shape a head. If you don't have this space the fly cannot be well finished.

Starting and Finishing a Fly

The beginning tier's problems start with the attempt to tie a fly without knowing how to begin or finish it. The jaws of most vises are shaped so that they grip the hook best when the hook is placed in the jaws at the bend of the hook. Burying the point of the hook in the jaws reduces the strength of the vise's grip.

Broken Thread

Few little disasters are as frustrating to the fly tier as the thread which breaks at a critical point in the tying sequence. The exact circumstances under which the thread breaks determine what can be done about it. Contain the damage created by the unraveling of the thread by clamping the thread with the hackle pliers. Frequently the other end of the break snaps back through the bobbin. Cut off the ragged end and rethread the bobbin.

Most often the thread breaks when hard pressure is applied to secure something like a wing butt. If the thread breaks at the hook, the unraveling end usually takes the wing with it. This requires unwinding the thread to a point at which the fly is secure. If the thread breaks at the bobbin or at a point in the tying sequence where it does not unravel, then it will usually be possible to secure the end without losing part of the fly.

In either case, secure the loose end of the thread and rethread the bobbin. Restart the thread on the fly, being sure to secure the end of the broken thread. Cut off the tag ends of both threads and proceed with the fly.

Handling Hair

Even tiers with some experience often have difficulty with hair. The problems generally begin when the hair is cut from the tail or hide. Always cut the hair from the base or edge of the tail or hide, and trim it close to the skin. This is not only an economical way to use the materials, but it also starts you out with the longest, most workable hairs.

In working hair, the first thing to do after cutting it from the hide is to remove the under-fur and short hairs. This under-fur fuzz looks awful, has no place in the fly, and prevents effective use of the hair stacker. Hold the hair near its tips and work the comb into it. Pull the comb through the butts of the hair, thus removing most of the under-fur. The bodkin is also useful to pick out strands of fuzz. Flick the butts of the hair with your forefinger to knock out loose hairs that are too short for the operation at hand.

Firmly grasp the very tips of the hairs with the thumb and forefinger of the left hand. Gently grasp the butts of the hairs with the right hand and, by pulling apart, remove the hairs which are not quite in position. Rematch the two groups of hairs, aligning their tips. Repeat this process as necessary. Place the hair in the stacker with the tips facing into the closed end. Smartly rap the stacker against your palm several times, thus aligning the tips of the hairs.

Throughout this process, remove any broken, off-color, or otherwise unsuitable hairs. The result of this effort should be a bundle of neatly aligned hair ready to use as a tail or wing.

Tails

Quite a few materials can be used for tails, but most dry flies employ hair or hackle fibers. Hackle fiber tails sometimes give people trouble. Keeping the tips even, especially when more than one group of fibers is involved, often presents a problem. Before proceeding with the attachment of the tail this problem needs to be resolved in the following manner. Stroke the hackle barbules back between thumb and forefinger of the right hand to align the tips. Hold the group of barbules firmly between the thumb and forefinger of the left hand to strip them off the hackle stem. Transfer the group of hackle barbules to the thumb and forefinger of the right hand and back again to the left hand to gather it together. Pick up a new group of hackle barbules and align their tips with the group already in hand. Continue this procedure until there are enough hackle fibers for the task.

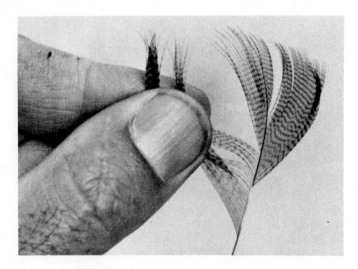 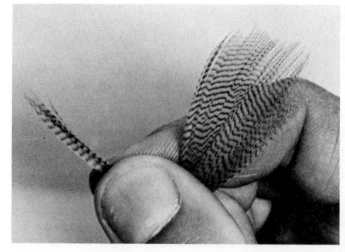

To properly secure a tail on a fly follow the outlined method. First decide the amount of material required, as outlined above. Hold the material between the thumb and forefinger of the left hand at the indicated point of attachment. Then catch a loop of thread loosely over the material to be secured between the fingers. Tighten with a firm but steady pull straight down. Catch a second loop and repeat the process. By holding the tail or other material in place on top of the hook while applying tension to the thread, the tendency for materials to roll off the hook is blocked.

Preparing Peacock for Quill Bodies

Quill bodies begin as a peacock eye; so it is wise to save the eyes from the peacock plumes you use. Select one or several of these eyes. It is not absolutely necessary, but it is a good idea to dampen the peacock eye prior to proceeding with the next step. Pour about half a cup of Purex or other household bleach into a bowl. Place the peacock eye in the bowl of bleach and swish it around. As you swish the eye in the bleach you will notice that the herl starts to turn a uniform brown. The flue will begin to strip off the herl as it dissolves, leaving only the stem. Continue to swish the eye around using your fingernails to help strip the flue. Remove the eye from the bleach bath and rinse it in a stream of cold water. Use your fingernails to work at stripping the flue from the quill. Usually at this stage most of the flue will be off the quill but it will be necessary to soak the quill again in the bleach. Since the bleach dissolves the quill stem as well as the flue (not as rapidly), it is necessary to pay attention and remove the eye from the bleach as soon as the flue is gone. Thoroughly rinse the stripped eye in running water after removing it from the bleach for the last time. Don't leave any trace of bleach in the eye because it will continue to dissolve the eye.

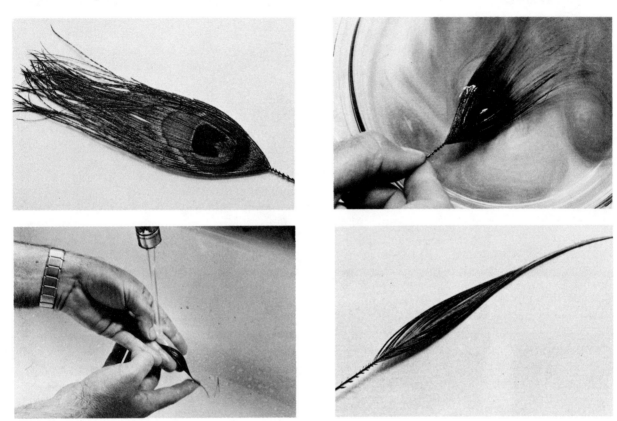

Repeat these steps with additional eyes as desired. It is difficult to work with more than six eyes at a time. The bleach becomes foul and ceases to work effectively after three eyes, necessitating its replacement. The need to keep track of what stage each eye is at puts a practical limit on how many eyes can be handled at one time.

Set the finished quill aside on an absorbent material to dry. The quills will dry stiff and become brittle, but let them dry out thoroughly before attempting to store them. The dried quills should be stored in an envelope or other protective container until you are ready to use them. Have a small dish of water available in which to soak the quill to restore and retain its flexibility when tying. The neatly segmented quill body is certainly one of the most naturalistic and effective of body materials.

Tying the Quill Body

Quill bodies are very effective and quite durable when correctly tied. With the thread at the tail position, tie in a strand of tan 3/0 mono-cord, using one turn of thread for the rib. Some may prefer to use gold wire for the rib, but I feel that thread is stronger. Tie in a single strand of peacock quill and wind the thread forward to the front of the body segment. Use close turns to make a smooth base for the quill, being sure to cover all of the tail and wing butts. Spread a layer of cement over the entire body area. Wind the quill into the wet cement, using open turns, thus leaving a small band of black showing between the turns. Tie the quill off with a single turn of thread. Now wind the ribbing thread onto each turn of the quill to reinforce it. Tie the rib off with two or three turns of thread and trim the excess. While lacquering the head after finishing the fly, add a layer of lacquer to the lamination of the body. Hair strands and hackle stems may also be used to form quill bodies. All quill bodies are improved by this process of multiple layering in cement.

Dubbed Fur Bodies

One technique basic to fly tying, which seems complicated and defeats many, is dubbing fur bodies. There are two keys to successfully dubbing fur bodies. The first key is the preparation of the basic fur ball. (A mini-blender reduces the repetitive labor of blending the fur for those who are tying a large number of fur bodied flies.)

Trim a clump of fur, clipping it close to the hide to avoid wastage. The fur has two components, the fur itself and the long "guard hairs." Pull the guard hairs out of the fur clump and discard them. Repeat the first two steps several times. If using a blender, place the fur in the blender and blend it. If hand blending, hold the fur with the fingers of the left hand and pull it apart with the right. Place the fur back together, pull it apart again from a different angle, and repeat this until the hair is well mixed. The result of this blending is a ball of fur ready for the actual process of dubbing a body.

The second key element in dubbing fur bodies is the dubbing process itself. Tease a strand of fur out of the fur ball. Practice will enable you to pull a consistent strand of the length required for the size fly. Lay the loose strand in the palm of the left hand and roll the strand with the forefinger of the right hand to compact the strand. Once the fur strand is prepared, set it aside temporarily and move on to the actual dubbing of the body (see page 79).

The process begins with the thread at the wing position. Pull several inches of thread off the bobbin and make it into a loop. Secure the loop to the hook and wind the thread toward the tail, carrying the base of the loop with it. End with the thread and the loop at the tail position. Continue to hold the loop open with one finger of the left hand. Return the tying thread to just behind the wing position. Varnish or wax the dubbing loop. Obviously, if your fingers become sticky it will be difficult to handle the fur. I prefer varnish to secure the dubbing fur because wax has always given me trouble. Lay the prepared fur strand between the two varnished strands of the loop. Twist the loop to form the fur into a yarn around the thread. Wind the dubbed yarn with close turns to form the body.

Peacock Herl Bodies

Peacock is one of the most important body materials. It is easy to make a poor peacock body, but only a little harder to make a good one. The key to a good peacock body is reinforcement.

Trim a strand of peacock herl from the stem. If the fly is a large one, or if the strands are particularly thin, then two or more may be required. Attach the peacock herl to the fly at the bend of the hook. End with the thread just behind the wing position. Wind the peacock with close turns. If this first pass produces a body of sufficient density, fine. If not, use open turns and wind the heel back to the tail and forward again. Tie off the peacock with two or three turns of the thread and cut off any excess herl. Using open turns, wind the thread back through the peacock to the tail. and then forward again, criss-crossing thread over the stem of the peacock herl. This reinforcement makes the body very durable.

Wings

Dry flies generally employ one of two types of wings. Those wings which lie down over the back of the fly have been described as "backwings" or "downwings." Downwings are commonly constructed of hair or a rolled wing quill. The other type of wing is the erect, which is generally a divided wing. Erect wings may be made of hair and wing quills, but are also commonly constructed from hackle points or duck flank feathers.

Downwings are attached to the hook in the same manner as tails. Rolled quill wings are a little different. The wing quill must be sprayed with Grumbacher Artist's Spray. This fixes the

24

individual fibers of the wing quill so that it is less likely to split when it is rolled over the body.

Erected wings fall into two classes which can be handled alike. Hackle point and erected quill wings are essentially similar, as are the flank feathers and hair wing pairs. A third sort of erected wing is the undivided wing used on parachute flies and some others. The erection process is essentially similar, but the wing is not divided at all.

The hackle point wing serves as the model for this discussion. Select the material for the wing. Hackle point wings should use feathers with shape and color patterns that are similar. Cut quill wing segments from opposite sides of previously paired wing quills. Match the tips of the material so that the natural curves bend away from each other. Prepare the hackle points by judging them for length while stroking the individual barbules away from the attachment point. There is no equivalent step for the quill wing.

Attach the wing to the hook as described for each type of fly. In most cases the order of construction requires the wing to be attached after the tail but before the body is formed, thus burying the wing butts under the body. After tying the body, erect the wings. Pull the wings erect and back between the thumb and forefinger of the left hand and place several turns of the thread immediately against the base of the wing to keep it erect. Quill wings require more turns here than hackle point wings because the increased density of material makes it more inclined to migrate forward. Build a slightly tapered base to prevent this tendency. Use the bodkin to separate the two halves of the wing. Then, holding the near wing segment with the thumb and forefinger of the left hand, take a single turn of thread between the wing segments going from the front to the back. As you come around behind the wing, shift your grip to the other wing segment, placing a second turn between the wings with the thread passing from behind to ahead of the wing. Place one or two more turns in front of the whole wing against its base. With one open turn, wind the thread behind the wing to the head of the body. Place a drop of cement between the bases of the divided wings to seal the area.

Hair and flank feather wings are very similar to each other. The actual erection and division of the two wing types is identical, but there are differences in the preparation of the material. Prepare the material for hair wings as previously described on page 21.

The typical flank feather has a rounded outline which requires that the material be aligned and stripped from the stem. As described for hackle-barbule tails, stroke the fibers of the flank feather back with the thumb and forefinger of the left hand to align their tips. Shift your grip to the right hand, enabling your left to firmly grip the aligned fibers. Then shift the right hand grip to the main body of the feather and strip the fibers from the stem. If more material is required, hold the already stripped fibers between thumb and forefinger of the left hand and match up the tips of the new material. Then strip the new material from the stem.

The order of construction requires that the wing be attached to the hook before the body is formed. Attach the wings using the technique already described. After completing the body, erect the wings. Pull the wings erect with the left thumb and forefinger, as before, and place several turns of thread against the base of the wing to hold it erect. Use the bodkin to divide the wing. If you hold the wing between the left thumb and forefinger in a bunch, the bodkin can be used to separate it into two equal segments.

Grasping the near wing segment between thumb and forefinger of the left hand, pass the thread from in front of the wing to behind the wing between the wing segments. Pick up the other wing segment between thumb and forefinger of the left hand and finish the figure 8 by crossing from behind the wing to in front of it. Repeat the figure 8 two or more times ending with the thread in front of the wing. Now start the thread between the wings as before, but make a complete clockwise turn around the base of the far wing segment. Make three complete clockwise close turns around the base of the wing segment to make a collar around it. As you end the last turn of the collar on the far wing the thread will be passing from front to rear between the two wing segments. Shift your left hand grip to the near wing and begin collaring it with counter-clockwise turns. Again, make this collar three turns wide.

Finish by making one more figure 8 between the wings and placing two more turns in front of the wing. Bring the thread around behind the wings to the end of the body position with a single open turn. Complete the wing process by placing a small drop of cement in the division of the wing to seal the figure 8's and the wing collars.

Hackles

The remaining major technique to master is the process of hackling a fly. The key to this is hackle selection and preparation. Dry fly hackle must have stiff barbules, but the stiffness is only partly associated with the webbing. Stroke the barbules back toward the butt of the feather. Those barbules which remain matted are not stiff enough. A noticeably soft feather should be saved for wet fly use. Bending the feather into an arc and brushing your upper lip with the tips of the barbules will give an additional check on the stiffness of the feather. Establish some sort of filing system to retrieve those feathers which are the wrong size for the fly.

Trim the barbules at the butt of the feather instead of stripping them, since most of the strength of the stem is in the outer shell. Dampening the stems of feathers will help prevent breakage. Most dry flies require two hackles. Face the feathers so that the dull sides, or backs, of the feathers face together and the shiny sides are out. One of the feathers will probably be longer than the other. Place this one in the back, so that the short one gets wound first. If only one hackle is required, face it so that the dull side faces you. Facing the hackle this way will build a broader base to float the fly.

Mastery of the basic techniques described in this chapter will enable you to tie literally hundreds of flies. Remember that the key elements stressed throughout this text are materials control and proportion. The weakest point that I see in amateur and professional flies alike is loose, bulky, sloppy construction resulting from a failure to manage the amount of material going into the fly. Failure to maintain proper proportion both causes and is caused by failure to control the materials.

Chapter III

Fishing and Tying
Stoneflies and Terrestrials

FISHERMEN are brought out of angling hibernation by news of the salmonfly hatch. They crowd the banks of many western rivers during May and June attempting to catch a trophy size trout. This is the hatch that brings the really big trout to the surface. More big trout are caught on dry flies during the salmonfly hatch than at any other time. These insects are really stoneflies (order *Plecoptera*), but they were named salmonflies because of their salmon orange color.

The most important western species of the stoneflies is *Pteronarcys californica*. This insect has a tangerine colored body with dark brown tail and heavily veined wings. The body length is almost two inches and the wing expanse is approximately four inches. Antennae length is nearly an inch. This specie is found from the Pacific Coast through the Rocky Mountain states.

Another important western species of the stoneflies is the *Acroneuria californica*, also called the golden stonefly or California salmonfly. Its body is a golden color and its wings are yellowish-brown. Body length is approximately one inch and its wing expanse is approximately one and one-half inches. Although this species is found in the Rocky Mountain states it is of primary importance on streams and rivers in California, Oregon and Washington.

The salmonfly and golden stonefly, like other species of stoneflies, prefer fast-flowing, well aerated water. Rocky stream bottoms are this insect's favorite habitat. Stoneflies are not found on streams and rivers having a silt bottom. Due to their inefficient gill systems, stoneflies cannot adapt to pollution and are found only in pure, fast-flowing streams.

The life cycle of stoneflies consists of egg, nymph and adult. The nymphal stage lasts from one year to three years depending on the species. The most important western species, *Pteronarcys californica*, has a nymphal stage of three years. The adult stage lasts from two to six weeks.

The salmonfly hatch or emergence takes place on western rivers mainly during May and June. A few rivers have a hatch lasting into July. The hatch takes place when salmonflies in the nymphal stage start a mass migration toward shore. Salmonflies emerge, unlike mayflies, by literally climbing out of the water onto the bank or onto rocks, logs, branches or anything that intercepts the water. During this nymphal migration, trout gorge themselves on nymphs tumbling along in the current.

Once the salmonfly reaches land, it splits out of its nymphal shuck, dries its wings and then flies to the shade of nearby trees and bushes. Here they stay until mating takes place. Female salmonflies lay their eggs by flying close to the water's surface and dipping their egg-laden abdomens into the water. During this period of egg laying, salmonflies are vulnerable to trout. After egg laying is complete some female salmonflies, due to post-coital exhaustion, fall into the stream. Salmonflies are also blown and washed into streams, creating additional surface feeding for trout. The rate of the upstream movement of the hatch is determined by how rapidly the water on a particular stream is warming up. Rapidly warming water means that the salmonfly hatch will move quickly upstream. Cold weather and slowly warming water conditions will, of course, slow down the upstream progress of the hatch.

The salmonfly hatch always moves upstream. In front of the head of the hatch it is best to use a stonefly nymph, fished as close to the bottom as possible, since the trout are keyed to intercepting the emerging nymphs trying to reach shore. Behind the head of the hatch trout quickly stop searching for migrating nymphs and begin to concentrate on salmonflies that are on the surface. Here is where the dry salmonfly imitation works best. Finding where the head of the hatch is located is not an easy matter. One method is to walk upstream looking for nymphal shucks on rocks along the shore and for adult salmonflies on streamside trees and bushes. When nymphal shucks and adults are no longer seen it is a good bet that you are ahead of the hatch and are in good stonefly nymph territory.

Salmonfly hatch dates are difficult to pinpoint. Set out below are the dates when the salmonfly hatch normally takes place on many important western rivers. Remember, these are approximate dates. They can vary significantly depending on water and weather conditions. Cold weather and high water normally mean the hatch will appear later than the dates given. Warm weather and low water will cause the hatch to take place earlier. The dates set out assume normal weather and water conditions. It is always a good idea to contact a local fly fishing shop for up-to-the-minute information before attempting to fish the salmonfly hatch.

Special thanks is owed to Randall Kaufmann of Portland, Oregon, author of the *American Nymph Fly Tying Manual* for hatch date information for Oregon's rivers; to Dick Anderson, owner of Missoula Streamside Anglers for hatch date information for some of Montana's waters; to Reverend Chuck Christopher of Gunnison, Colorado for information concerning the Gunnison River; and Chuck Fothergill, owner of Chuck Fothergill's Outdoor Sportsman in Aspen, Colorado, for hatch information for Colorado waters.

RIVERS AND DATES OF STONEFLY HATCHES

Rock Creek (Montana): The salmonfly hatch starts around June 10 and finishes by July 10. High, discolored water can make dry fly fishing impossible during the start of the hatch. The water usually clears around July 1. There are several Rock Creeks in Montana. The stream referred to here is located near Missoula, Montana and is a tributary of the Clark's Fork of the Columbia.

Clark's Fork of the Columbia (Montana): The hatch starts around Missoula, Montana by June 10, moves upstream and is finished by July 10. The hatch doesn't proceed much past the confluence of the Clark's Fork and Rock Creek. High water is often a problem at the start of the hatch.

Big Hole River (Montana): The hatch lasts from June 1 to June 20. High water is often a problem during the entire hatch.

Madison River (Montana): The hatch takes place June 15 to July 15. The hatch starts below Beartrap Canyon west of Bozeman and moves upstream toward West Yellowstone. The portion of the Madison River inside Yellowstone Park does not experience much of a hatch. The water is usually high and discolored at the start of the hatch. The water clears by July 1.

Yellowstone River (Montana and Wyoming): The hatch starts below Livingston, Montana around June 25 and finishes at Canyon Village in Yellowstone National Park by August 1. The hatch moves through Gardiner, Montana around July 1. High water is usually a problem at the start of the hatch. The water normally doesn't clear until July 1.

Gardiner River (Montana and Wyoming): This is a short hatch on a very short river. The hatch normally starts around July 1 and ends by July 7. The river has usually cleared by the start of the hatch.

Green River (Wyoming): The hatch starts around June 1 and lasts until June 21. High water is often a problem. The best hatch occurs around Pinedale, Wyoming.

Henry's Fork of the Snake River (Idaho): The hatch starts May 15 and ends by June 7. The water is often high but clear.

Colorado River (Colorado): Salmonflies, even the large *Pteronarcys*, are called willow flies in Colorado. The willow fly hatch starts on the Colorado River around June 7 and lasts until around July 1. High water is often a problem at the start of the hatch.

Gunnison River (Colorado): The *Pteronarcys* has been very nearly eliminated on the Gunnison, courtesy of the Corps of Army Engineers, though local sportsmen are attempting to re-establish the survivors. A fair but scattered hatch of *Acroneuria* occurs between June 21 and July 21. The stonefly hatch is normally accompanied by heavy caddis hatches. The river is clear by the start of the hatch.

Roaring Fork River (Colorado): The hatch dates are from May 25 to June 15. The water can be high and discolored for much of the hatch.

Frying Pan River (Colorado): The hatch is from June 7 to June 21. High water is often a problem.

Deschutes River (Oregon): The hatch starts in the lower river below Pelton Dam by May 25 and ends by mid June. The upper river above Pelton Dam to the headwaters experience a salmonfly hatch starting around June 1 and lasting two to three weeks. Water is high but usually clear by the start of the hatch. This river probably has the best hatch in Oregon.

Williamson River (Oregon): The hatch usually starts around May 15 and lasts until late June depending on elevation. This river has a very steep gradient and hence exceedingly swift water.

Crooked River (Oregon): This is a small river and has at best a fair hatch. The hatch starts around May 15 and lasts to the second week of June. Usually the water is high, but clears during the hatch period. *Warning: The area near the river is lousy with rattlesnakes.*

North Fork of the Umpqua River (Oregon): The hatch usually starts around June 1, lasting until June 15. The hatch sould be fished above Togetee, Oregon. Hatches below this point tend to be sparse. The South Fork of the Umpqua River has only a marginal hatch. Discoloration is usually not a problem during the hatch period.

Rogue River (Oregon): The hatch on Oregon's most famous river starts near the mouth around May 15 and moves upstream, ending by the end of June. On the Rogue the hatch does progress upstream but it is not as dependable and predictable as are the hatches on the famous Montana streams. High water is often a problem at the start of the hatch. The Rogue is primarily a steelhead and salmon river with only relatively small resident rainbow trout in the 10 to 13 inch class.

Metolius River (Oregon): The hatch starts by June 1 lasting until the first week of July. The water is high but usually clear for the start of the hatch period.

Klamath River (California): The hatch starts above Copco Lake around May 21 and lasts until June 15. *Warning: Watch out for sudden fluctuation in water levels when fishing this section. Flow changes are caused by power releases from Johnny Boyle Dam upstream in Oregon. You can get drowned if you are not extremely careful.* The water is usually clear for the hatch.

Hat Creek (California): The hatch usually starts around May 15 and ends the first week in June. Salmonfly hatches have been known to last into July on this creek. The water is usually clear during the entire hatch period.

EFFECTIVE SALMONFLY IMITATIONS AND PRESENTATION

There are several patterns designed to imitate the adult salmonfly. Patterns all the way from the Bucktail Caddis to the Sofa Pillow will catch fish. We have found after a lot of experimentation with other patterns that Bird's Golden Stonefly works best when attempting to imitate the golden (*Acroneuria californica*) variety of salmonfly. Parks' Salmonfly with its tangerine body and dark-brownish wings is my choice when attempting to imitate the large *Pteronarcys californica* hatch.

Other effective salmonfly imitations are the Dark Stone, Denny's Special, Deschutes Demon, Dick's Sofa Pillow, Giant Stonefly, Golden Stone, Jughead, Montana Bucktail and Stephenson's Fluttering Stonefly. (Dressings for these patterns are set out in the Pattern Directory at the back of the book.)

The best method of presenting a salmonfly imitation is to cast upstream close to the shore. When fishing these large flies, short casts work best. The cast should be made *close* to the bank, particularly under overhanging trees and bushes. Salmonflies are frequently blown or fall into the stream from streamside vegetation. Trout tend to take up feeding stations near the bank in order to intercept salmonflies entering the water as well as salmonfly nymphs migrating to shore. It is normally a waste of time to fish salmonfly imitations in the slow water of deep pools. It is best to concentrate your effort in fast riffle areas.

On most western streams and rivers, the water is normally high and slightly discolored for much of the salmonfly hatch, making it possible to use much heavier leader tippets than are possible when fishing in low clear water. I recommend that you use at least 1X or 2X tippet materials. Big trout are brought to the surface by the salmonfly hatch and it is best to be prepared.

Salmonfly imitations, like the natural insect they represent, are large flies requiring a heavy line to turn them over. I recommend that you use at least a six weight line and preferably a seven or eight weight line. Keeping the leader short, seven and a half feet or under, will also help with turn over. When using large flies and heavy lines, a long rod is a definite advantage. I prefer at least an eight and a half to nine foot rod for fishing the salmonfly hatch.

Small Stoneflies: Small stoneflies in hook sizes 12 to 18 look much like mayflies in the air. Many fishermen have fished a mayfly hatch all day only to discover later that the hatch was actually of small stoneflies. This points out the importance of collecting a sample before starting to fish. Remember that small stoneflies, like their big brother the salmonfly, prefer streams with rocky or gravel bottoms. Well-aerated pure water is essential to their existence.

There are several species of small yellow stoneflies that hatch in swift, gravel bottomed western streams. Some yellow stones emerge midstream like mayflies while others crawl onto the land like salmonflies. These insects have yellow bodies and legs. Wings are white with a tinge of lemon color. Their size is best matched by hook sizes 14 to 16. The hatch normally takes place in the Rocky Mountain States during July and August. Little yellow stones usually hatch during June and July in California, Oregon and Washington.

Bird's Stonefly tied in the smaller sizes is an effective imitation for little yellow stones. Small yellow bodied Humpys also work well to match the small yellow stonefly hatch. The Grizzly Wulff is another effective imitation. Even mayfly imitations like the Light Cahill will often work. These flies are best fished over riffle areas on streams that have rocky or gravel bottoms.

Green, olive and black bodied stoneflies also produce hatches. However, none of these species is as important as the little yellow stonefly. Small Humpys tied with an underbody color to match the particular color of the hatch are effective imitations.

TERRESTRIALS

Land born insects such as grasshoppers, ants, crickets and beetles are known as terrestrial insects. During certain times of the season, terrestrials make up a significant part of the trout's diet.

The most important terrestrials from the western fly fisherman's point of view are the grasshopper and the black ant.

Grasshopper season in the West usually starts around the middle of July. Grasshoppers are land born and are not aquatic insects. They get into the water by accident. Their presence in the water is caused by inadvertently jumping into the water, being blown in by strong winds, or by being washed in, usually by violent summer thunder storms.

Grasshoppers that find their way into the water are usually found close to shore. Grasshopper imitations should normally be fished by casting upstream and working the fly along the current line closest to the opposite bank. Dead drift often works well, but I prefer to occasionally twitch a grasshopper imitation as it floats along. Grasshoppers create quite a commotion when they fall into the water. A twitching motion imparted to your imitation signals to the trout the presence of a grasshopper in distress.

Another method of presentation is to cast your grasshopper fly upstream and across onto the opposite bank. Then slowly pull your fly from the bank into the water. This method is very effective when trout are keyed to grasshoppers entering the water from the bank. Do not try to pull the fly off the bank by lifting your rod tip. This will invariably cause your fly to get hooked on the bank. The best method is to point your rod tip directly at your fly and then pull the fly line slowly by hand straight towards you. Don't create an angle or arch between you and your fly or it will become snagged on the bank.

The best time to fish a grasshopper imitation is after midday. Grasshoppers, like other insects, are cold blooded and do not get active until their bodies have been warmed by the sun. Grasshopper activity quits in late afternoon when the air temperature cools. Warm windy days usually produce the best grasshopper fishing. Winds account for more grasshoppers in the water than any other factor. Grasshopper fishing is best in streams surrounded by grassy meadows rather than those running through timbered canyons. Normally the west side of a stream that flows north and south is the best side to fish a grasshopper or any terrestrial imitation. This is because in most places in the Northern Hemisphere the prevailing winds are from the west. Grasshoppers near the west bank are blown toward the stream. Grasshoppers near the east bank are blown away from the bank.

Our favorite hopper imitation for fishing rough, fast water is the heavy hackled Joe's Hopper. Even if the trout are not hitting grasshoppers, this fly, tied in small sizes, serves as a good caddis imitation and often trout mistake this imitation for a small golden stone. For smooth flat water, where trout tend to be more selective, our favorite hopper patterns are Dave's Hopper and the Deer Head Hopper. Both of these patterns sit lower in the water than the Joe's Hopper, producing a more realistic silhouette. The dressing for Dave's Hopper and the Deer Head Hopper are listed in the Pattern Directory at the back of the book.

It is often difficult to determine when trout are feeding on ants. Ants normally drift in the surface film and are difficult to see. Trout literally inhale them without creating a perceptible rise. Occasionally ants float on the surface with their wings showing. During this time ants are often mistaken for mayflies by the fisherman. However, mayfly imitations seldom fool the trout because the body silhouette of the ant and mayfly are much different. Remember to collect a sample before you start fishing. No matter how well you think you know a river, often you will be fooled.

Ants, like grasshoppers, get into the water by accident. Wind and sudden storms account for most ants present in the water. A size 16 Coachman Trude is sometimes effective when attempting to imitate an ant.

Ants are fished much like a grasshopper. However, if you impart a twitching motion to your ant imitation, do it much more subtly than when fishing a hopper. Due to their small size, ants can be blown far out into a river. Accordingly, it is best to start fishing an ant imitation close to the shore and gradually work it out. Feeding lanes for ants can be over a much wider area than the feeding lanes for grasshoppers. It is not often that you will use an ant imitation, but when trout are feeding on this terrestrial, an ant imitation many times is the only fly that will work.

IMPORTANT POINTS TO REMEMBER

1. Salmonflies are large insects. Body length can be one to two inches and wing expanse can be up to four inches.

2. The salmonfly hatch takes place on most western rivers during May and June. Consult the text for the rivers near your area for exact dates.

3. Salmonflies emerge by literally climbing out of the water. During this migration, trout gorge themselves on stonefly nymphs.

4. Salmonfly hatches always move upstream.

5. The head of the hatch can be found by walking upstream and finding the point where adult salmonflies are no longer seen on streamside trees or bushes and nymphal shucks are no longer seen on rocks near the shore.

6. Fish stonefly nymph imitations ahead of the hatch and dry fly imitations below the head of the hatch.

7. Bird's Golden Stonefly is the most effective imitation when attempting to match the golden stonefly or California salmonfly (*Acroneuria californica*). Parks' Salmonfly works best when matching the very large salmonfly (*Pteronarcys californica*).

8. Dry salmonfly imitations should be fished close to the bank. Riffle areas and under overhanging trees and bushes are especially good places to fish.

9. Small stoneflies look a lot like mayflies in the air. Always collect a sample.

10. Small yellow stoneflies are the most prevalent of the small stoneflies. Bird's Stonefly tied in the appropriate size is a good imitation. A yellow bodied Humpy will also work well for the hatch.

11. Grasshoppers are best fished tight against the bank. Imparting a twitching motion signals to the trout that a grasshopper is in distress. The west side of a stream or river is usually the best side to fish a terrestrial.

12. Grasshoppers are best fished during midday after these cold blooded insects become active.

13. Grasshoppers are the most prevalent on streams with grassy meadows.

14. Our favorite hopper pattern for rough, fast water is the Joe's Hopper. We prefer Dave's Hopper or the Deer Head Hopper for smooth flat water.

15. Ants are best fished close to shore, but can range further out into the water than grasshoppers. The dead drift is the best method of fishing an ant imitation.

BIRD'S STONEFLY

CAL Bird devised this pattern to represent *Acroneuria Californica*, the golden stonefly. We have also found it to be an effective imitation of the numerous *Alloperla*, little yellow stones. This pattern is very buoyant in the smaller sizes and it casts a very realistic silhouette.

   This fly is merely a design approach, not an absolute. The dressing for the Golden Stone can be readily modified to fit circumstances on streams which have good hatches of differently colored stoneflies. All you have to do is change the body color, hackle color, wing color and size to conform to your observations.

HOOK:	9671, sizes 10-16; most used, sizes 12-14.
THREAD:	Yellow 3/0 mono-cord.
TAIL:	Monofilament dyed brown (or hackle stems); monofilament is available from Dan Bailey.
BODY:	Yellow floss.
RIB:	Brown hackle tied palmer and trimmed.
WING:	Light brown bucktail.
HACKLE:	Brown saddle hackle trimmed to shape.
ANTENNAE:	Dyed monofilament (same as tails).

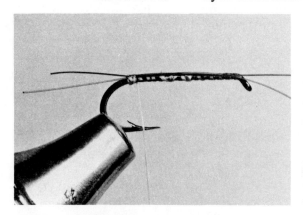

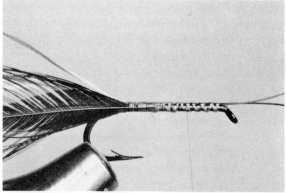

1. The tails are made of monofilament dyed brown, though stripped hackle stems may be substituted. Face the natural curves of the two strands of monofilament so that they bend away from each other, and attach them to the hook with two or three turns of the thread.

2. Attach a length of yellow floss to the hook for the body. Select a large brown feather for the palmered hackle rib and prepare it as usual. Secure it to the hook and then wind the thread forward.

32

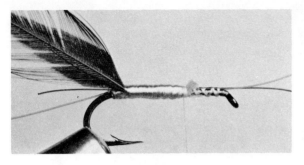

3. Wind the body floss, starting with one complete turn behind the ribbing feather. Tie off the body with two or three turns of the thread and trim off any excess floss.

4. Wind the ribbing feather, making one complete turn of the feather at the tail of the fly where it is tied in and with closely spaced open turns wind it the length of the body. Tie it off with a couple turns of the thread and trim off any excess.

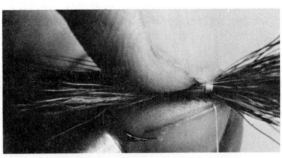

5. Picking up the ribbing hackle fibers between thumb and forefinger of the left hand, comb them up above the body of the fly. Hold with the thumb and forefinger of the right hand and repeat this process until you have the hackle gathered above the top of the fly. Trim this hackle fairly close and parallel to the body, leaving a uniform stubble all around the fly.

6. The wing should extend to the tip of the tail when attached with two or three turns of the thread. Flatten the wing material and spread it out over the back of the fly with your thumb and take a couple more turns of the thread to secure the wing in the spread position.

7. Trim the butt of the wing, leaving a slant facing toward the eye of the fly. Be careful not to trim off the antennae.

8. Select two brown saddle hackles; trim and prepare them as usual. Dampen the stems and attach the feathers to the hook. Duco the wing butt before finishing securing the wing and hackle butts. End with the thread at the head position.

9. Wind the two hackles one at a time, building up a close dense hackling. Secure each hackle with one or two turns and trim off their points. Shape the head, whip finish, and lacquer.

10. Trim the hackle flat on top and bottom, ending with the hackle only extending from the sides of the fly. Square off the ends of the hackle on the sides of the fly

PARKS' SALMONFLY

THE Parks' Salmonfly was first tied in 1954 by my father, Merton Parks. The current imitation for the *Pteronarcys Californica* was the Sofa Pillow, which was not satisfactory. The squirrel tail and red floss used in the Sofa Pillow did not produce the right color tones nor the floatability needed for a salmonfly imitation.

My father started from scratch to create a satisfactory salmonfly. The heavy bucktail tail gives floatability. Bucktail's reddish brown tones approximate those of the natural's body. Tangerine orange yarn further sets the color tone for the body and, when ribbed with trimmed palmer, shows the segmentation of the natural. The dark brown hackle finishes the fly and simulates the legs of the natural. Since that time, many of these ideas have been translated into various "improved" Sofa Pillows.

Whatever you call it, it remains one of the best salmonfly imitations going. The Golden Stones, *Acroneuria Californica*, having golden yellow body tones and lighter wings are easily represented by making appropriate changes in the colors used for body, wing and hackle. The design philosophy of this fly can be readily adapted to represent any of the major stonefly species.

HOOK:	9671, sizes 4-8.
THREAD:	Black A mono-cord.
TAIL:	Brown bucktail.
BODY:	Tangerine orange yarn.
RIB:	Clipped brown hackle tied palmer.
WING:	Brown bucktail.
HACKLE:	Dark brown saddle hackle.

1. The tail of this large fly should be quite heavy to help float the fly and serve as a body extension. Secure the tail with four turns of the thread and trim the butt of the tail, leaving a slant facing forward.

2. Attach the body yarn with three turns of the thread. Prepare a large dark brown hackle for the palmered rib of the fly and attach the ribbing feather with one or two turns of the thread. Using close turns, secure the tail butt, the butt of the body yarn, and the butt of the ribbing feather simultaneously. The wing position should be halfway between the point of the hook and the eye of the fly.

3. Wind the body yarn, making the first turn of the yarn behind the ribbing feather. Continue the close turns of the yarn. Keep the yarn taut at all times. Finish winding the body, tie it off with two or three turns of the thread, and trim.

4. Wind the ribbing feather with one complete turn at the butt and use open turns toward the eye of the fly. Tie the ribbing feather off with three turns of the thread.

5. Trim the hackle to a length about three-fourths that of the hook gape.

6. The wing tip extends exactly as far as the tail beyond the end of the hook. Secure the wing with four turns of thread. Trim the butt of the wing at a slant.

7. Face the two hackle feathers so that the inside curves of these feathers face each other, dull sides together and shiny sides facing out. Attach the hackles with two turns at the same point where the wing has been secured to the hook.

8. Secure the wing butt with several tight turns. Wind the hackles and secure them with one or two turns of the tying thread. Guard the hackles with your fingers by using the thumb and first two fingers to stroke the hackle back from the eye while you are shaping the head. Whip finish and cement.

BUCKTAIL CADDIS

THE Bucktail Caddis originated in the Pacific Northwest and has been very popular for many years. I first saw this fly in 1955, but I understand that it had already proven itself for several seasons before that. There are obvious similarities between this fly and the Parks' Salmonfly. The problems which the Bucktail Caddis solve are those presented by the requirement to represent stoneflies, caddisflies and grasshoppers on rough water.

The fly has been adapted by shops all over the West to meet their local needs. Using a long shank hook makes it a better stonefly. The body, hackle and wing colors have been altered to cover the entire spectrum of natural tones, but the fly is still usually identified as a Bucktail Caddis, Caddis Buck, Elk Hair Caddis or some name of this sort which reveals its ancestry.

HOOK:	94840, sizes 8-14.
THREAD:	Black 3/0 mono-cord.
TAIL:	Brown hackle fibers — very heavy.
BODY:	Yellow yarn.
RIB:	Brown hackle.
WING:	Light bucktail (coarse hair from base of tail).

1. Strip a sizable bundle of stiff brown hackle barbules from the stem of a feather and attach it to the hook for the tail. Trim the butt of the tail at a slant as shown.

2. Attach the body yarn and select a brown saddle hackle for the palmered rib. Wind the body, starting with one turn of the yarn behind the ribbing feather. Tie off the yarn with three turns of thread.

37

3. The first turn of the ribbing feather should be a tight turn at the rear of the fly. The remainder should be corkscrew turns. Tie off the hackle with three turns of thread and trim.

4. The wing on this fly extends only to the bend of the hook. Attach the wing with four turns of the thread. Trim the butt of the wing at a slant, pack it with Duco, and then secure the wing butt while forming the head. Whip finish and cement.

BLACK ANT

FISH seldom become selectively keyed to ants due simply to a relative lack of opportunity. When they do, it is imperative to have an effective ant imitation. The ant is a terrestrial insect which doesn't ordinarily get into the water in large numbers. The swarming flight phase of the ant's life cycle is the most likely source of ants. This is the period when ants are most subject to the vagaries of wind and rain. However, a certain number of accidents befall small numbers of ants throughout the season.

I have tied a Black Ant but the same design applies if the ants you intend to imitate are red ants. Use natural bucktail or dyed hair of the appropriate reddish brown color and brown hackle. The flying ant of either type can be represented by adding wings, using blue dun hackle points. The popular fur ants are essentially the same, but make the abdomen and thorax of dubbed fur instead of hair.

HOOK:	94838, sizes 16-20.
THREAD:	Black 6/0 pre-waxed.
BODY:	Black bucktail.
HACKLE:	Charcoal neck hackle.

1. From a dyed black bucktail, trim a few hairs — not very much as this is a small fly — to make the body of the ant. Secure the bucktail at the tail position.

2. Wind the thread over the butts to get them secured firmly to the hook. You can use several turns here, as you will want to build up the body anyway. Build up a hump of thread at the back of the fly. The proportion of the ant requires that the rear body segment be larger than the forward segment.

3. Lacquer the thread underbase at the rear of the fly before pulling the hair over to make the rear body segment. Gather the hair up into a single tight bundle and pull it over the back of the fly. You may let it slide down around the sides before securing it.

4. Select a single charcoal feather. The curve or dull side should face towards you.

5. Now wind just a couple of turns of the hackle in the center of the fly. Use one turn of the thread to secure the hackle. Then pull up the body hair and tie the hackle off underneath the body.

6. With the hackle tied off, build up a second small hump with the tying thread in the front to make the second body segment of the fly.

7. Once again place a drop of lacquer on the thread underbody before pulling the hair over. Pull the hair down to make the second body segment, which should be shorter than the first body segment.

8. Shape the head and whip finish. Lacquer the head and the body. Place the completed ant on a pin to dry.

JOE'S HOPPER

NOT only is the Joe's Hopper one of the oldest grasshopper imitations, it remains one of the best. Originating in the Midwest, it is sometimes referred to as the Michigan Hopper. The major difficulty with the fly is the reliance on mottled turkey, which is now a rare material. However, the tier can use pheasant tail or deer hair as a substitute material.

HOOK:	9671, sizes 6-14.
THREAD:	Black 3/0 mono-cord.
TAIL:	Red hackle fibers.
BODY:	Yellow yarn.
RIB:	Brown hackle tied palmer and trimmed.
WING:	Mottled turkey quill (pheasant or deer hair).
HACKLE:	Brown and grizzly hackle mixed.

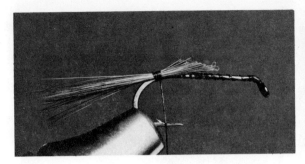

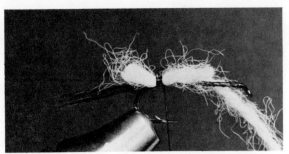

1. Strip red hackle fibers from a large feather with stiff barbules for the tail. Attach these to the hook with three turns of the thread.

2. Form a small loop in the end of the body yarn and attach it to the hook. Trim the butt so that the yarn does not extend past the mid-point of the hook.

3. Select a large brown feather for the palmer rib. Wind the body yarn, starting with a complete turn behind the ribbing feather. Wind the ribbing feather.

4. Trim the hackle, leaving an even stubble all around the hook. Clip out the loop in the body yarn.

5. Treat a mottled turkey wing quill with Grumbacher's Fixative to inhibit splitting when the feather is rolled. Cut a segment from the quill twice as wide as the hook gape. Roll the wing over the hook as shown and secure it.

6. Select one brown and one grizzly hackle. Wind each hackle. Trim the hackle points and whip finish the fly.

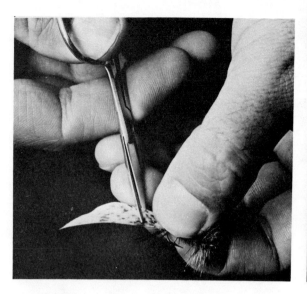
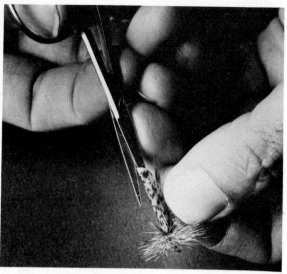

7. Remove the fly from the vise. Trim the tip of the wing into a smooth curve.

8. Slit up the back of the wing with the scissors. Cement the head and place the fly on a pin to dry.

Chapter IV

Fishing and Tying
Rough Water Attractor Flies

MANY western streams and rivers are characterised by rough, broken, swift water. This kind of water works to the advantage of the fly fisherman. The trout, because of the swift current, has a very short time to examine an artificial and the broken surface obscures the trout's vision of the offering. This is the kind of water where the fly fisherman doesn't have to worry about exact hatch matching.

What is needed for rough water dry fly fishing is a dry fly that sits high on the water, is easy to see and has a general resemblance to many different kinds of insects. Flies that meet these requirements are labeled *rough water attractor flies.*

In order to successfully fish rough water attractor patterns, you must acquire three fundamental skills: First, you must learn which attractor pattern to use for any given fishing situation; second, it is imperative to learn how to read water well; and finally it is important to learn how to perform certain casting techniques which are designed to accomplish a drag free presentation. Drag is the single most important problem to presenting the fly properly. I will elaborate on each of the fundamental skills in turn.

SELECTING THE RIGHT ROUGH WATER ATTRACTOR FLY

Two different theories exist to explain the effectiveness of attractor dry fly patterns. One theory contends that attractor patterns, while not being specifically imitative, have a close enough resemblance to many different insect forms as to be recognized as food by the trout. The other theory holds that attractor patterns hold some magic ingredient which attracts fish independent of any deliberate attempt to masquerade as food. Those fishermen subscribing to the latter theory point to studies showing that trout, for no apparent reason, are attracted to the color red. While no one has had a debriefing interview with a caught trout, it may well be that fish are attracted to the color red because they associate that color with the blood of a wounded fish. If this proves to be the reason for the attraction, then it is not the inherent nature of the color red which is the attractor, but the association red has with food.

I subscribe to the first theory. When the popular attractor patterns are carefully analyzed it becomes apparent that each pattern is suggestive of one or more specific insects that make up an important aspect of the diet of the trout. It is my belief that it is this general resemblance which causes trout to strike attractor flies. Take the Royal Wulff for example; if this pattern is fished without wings, the number of strikes decreases dramatically due to the fact that the pattern no longer creates the upright wing silhouette of the mayfly. The fish that still strike the wingless Royal Wulff probably do so because the fly appears to them as some sort of a caddis bouncing around on the surface. If the next step is taken and the hackle is removed so that you are now fishing a fly that is essentially floating peacock with a red band and a brown tail, few if any strikes will occur. This is because the fly no longer resembles an insect food form. If the fish were attracted to the fly independent of its resemblance to food then removing features of the fly that make it resemble food would not necessarily reduce the number of strikes.

Rough water attractor flies fit into three categories: those attractor patterns with upright wings (represented by the Royal Wulff and Humpy), those attractor patterns tied with a single downwing (represented by the Coachman Trude), and those attractor patterns tied with a single fore and aft hackle and no wings (represented by the Renegade and Buzz Hackle).

Each category of attractor patterns is best used for a different fishing situation. When to use the different attractor flies is set out below in the rough water attractor fly rules.

ROUGH WATER ATTRACTOR FLY RULES

1. **Mayfly Streams:** If the stream on which you are fishing has a predominantly mayfly population, attractor flies like the Royal Wulff and Humpy that have upright wings resembling the mayfly should be used. Trout in predominantly mayfly streams key to upright winged insects, so it is logical to use an attractor pattern with upright wings. This is not to say that a downwing attractor fly or a fore and aft attractor fly won't work; it merely points out that if the trout are looking for upright winged insects, an attractor pattern with upright wings will catch more fish than patterns tied with downwings or fore and aft style.

2. **Caddisfly Streams:** If the stream on which you are fishing has a predominantly caddis population, then an attractor pattern that has a downwing suggestive of the adult caddis works best. The downwing Coachman Trude is always my first choice on this kind of stream. Fore and aft hackled attractor patterns also work well on this kind of stream. The Renegade and Buzz Hackle have the underwater appearance of being downwinged. The numerous hackle points touching the water give these flies a fluttering effect imitative of the adult caddis dancing on the water.

3. **Mayfly-Caddisfly Combination Streams:** On streams that have a significant population of both mayflies and caddisflies, the best attractor pattern that I have found is the Humpy. In my opinion the upright winged Humpy does a better job representing the downwinged caddisfly than some of the downwinged attractor patterns. Part of the rationale behind this is that the natural dun mayfly always appears to the trout as an upright winged insect. Caddisflies, on the other hand, appear to the trout at different times as either an upwinged or downwinged insect. Caddisflies, when at rest on the water, hold their wings in the downwinged position. When fluttering on or near the water surface this insect holds its wings upright. Therefore, the upright winged attractor patterns like the Humpy always present the correct wing silhouette for the dun mayfly and the correct wing silhouette for the fluttering caddis.

On the other hand, a downwinged attractor pattern like the Coachman Trude always creates an incorrect wing silhouette for matching mayfly duns and for representing fluttering caddis. In short, on a combination mayfly-caddis stream, an upright winged attractor pattern is going to present the correct wing silhouette more of the time than a downwinged attractor pattern. I prefer the Humpy over the Royal Wulff on this kind of combination stream because I find that the muted colors of the Humpy are more in keeping with the muted colors of the caddisfly and mayfly than are the bright colors of the Royal Wulff.

   4. Caddis-Stonefly Combinations: If the stream on which you are fishing has a predominantly caddisfly and stonefly population, or there are lots of grasshoppers getting into the water, then downwinged attractor patterns or fore and aft attractor patterns suggestive of these insects work best. My first choice in this kind of fishing situation is the Coachman Trude followed by the Buzz Hackle and the Renegade.

   5. Attractor patterns are best used on rough, broken, swift water when a hatch is NOT taking place. When a hatch is on you will normally catch more trout by selecting a fly pattern that is more of an exact imitation of the specific insect on which the trout are feeding than are attractor patterns. An exception to this rule is on a stream or river that has very fast, rough, heavy water. Sometimes on this kind of water I use an attractor pattern or a heavily dressed traditional pattern during a hatch because the sparsely hackled imitative patterns such as the Quill Gordon, Light Cahill, and Paradun are too easily drowned by the fast heavy current.

   6. If you are not sure of the predominant insect hatch on the stream you are fishing, and the water is rough and broken, then I suggest that you start out with the Humpy. It has a general resemblance to many different kinds of insects. This fly, especially when tied in smaller sizes, works well as a mayfly imitation. When tied with a yellow underbody it is an effective imitation for the small yellow stoneflies that make up significant hatches on many western streams. Ted Fay, a well known guide on the upper Sacramento River in Northern California, uses the Humpy tied in hook sizes 6 to 8 with an orange underbody to imitate the large orange caddisfly that hatches on the upper Sacramento River and many other western streams in October. The Humpy has the same muted color characteristics of most caddisflies and is a dynamite pattern when caddisflies are fluttering on the surface.

   In order to make the best utilization of the rough water attractor fly rules, the fly fisherman should first determine the predominant insect on which the trout are feeding. Once the predominant insect food source is known then it is easy to determine into which category (mayfly, caddisfly, mayfly-caddisfly combination, caddisfly-stonefly combination) the rough water stream falls.

   The best method of determining what the trout are eating is to get a sample. One method of collecting a sample is to first catch a trout and by use of a stomach pump ascertain what the trout has been eating (methods of collecting a sample are discussed in detail in the chapter *Mayfly Imitations*).

   If the sample consists primarily of mayfly insect food forms and few, if any, caddis forms then the stream should be tentatively classified as a mayfly stream and an upwinged attractor pattern used. If, on the other hand, the sample reveals a fairly equal mixture of caddis and mayfly insect forms then a tentative classification of a mayfly-caddis stream is warranted. In short, the sample must be analyzed to determine into which category the rough water stream falls. It is a good idea to take several samples before a definite stream and fly classification is made.

   Although collecting a sample is the best way to determine the predominant insect on which the trout are feeding, I know that many times the fly fisherman gets excited, myself included, and starts fishing without collecting a sample. Below are some generalizations which are helpful in determining into which category a particular stream fits. Remember that these generalizations are subject to exceptions.

   Most western spring creeks, especially those with alkaline rich water, tend to be predominantly mayfly streams. Streams like Armstrong and Nelson Spring Creeks, Henry's Fork of the Snake River and Silver Creek in Idaho are all mayfly waters.

   Most rain and snow fed streams, especially those located in the Rocky Mountains, tend to be predominantly caddisfly streams. Often these streams have sporadic mayfly hatches, but normally the greatest insect biomass is made up of caddisflies. I know of very few fast moving streams or rivers in Colorado, Wyoming and Montana that are not predominantly caddisfly water.

   There seems to be a correlation between water speed and insect population. As stream water

44

speed increases, the likelihood of the predominant insect biomass being caddisflies or stoneflies increases. Conversely, as stream water speed slows down the likelihood of the predominant insect biomass being of caddisflies or stoneflies decreases and the likelihood of the predominant biomass being mayflies increases. The Yellowstone River is a good example of this phenomenon. In the slower parts of the Yellowstone River near Fishing Bridge and in Hayden Valley in Yellowstone Park, good mayfly hatches take place. In the faster sections of the river near the town of Gardiner, Montana, mayfly hatches are at best sporadic, with the caddisfly being the predominant insect. Fast rough water normally suggests a predominantly caddisfly stream. Slow meadow water or a spring creek usually adds up to a predominantly mayfly stream.

READING THE WATER

The subject of reading the water seems to defeat more fishermen than it should. Study after study indicates that 90% of the fish are caught by 10% of the fishermen. One of the principal reasons for the failure of the majority of the fishermen to join the successful 10% is a failure to understand the principles of reading the water.

The bottom line is that fish must have, in common with other beasts, a bedroom and a kitchen. The kitchen is the cafeteria line of a current. The bedroom is slower water where a fish can rest, although the bedroom is never dead water. Dead water holds neither food nor adequate oxygen. The closer the bedroom is to the kitchen the better a fish likes it. Throw in physical cover such as overhanging rocks or vegetation and you have a prime target.

Behind Rocks: Rocks in a stream or river create a barrier or buffer to the current. The current is parted as it goes around a rock, leaving slack water immediately behind the rock. This slack water provides the trout with shelter from the current. A nearby source of food is provided by the current lines on either side of the slack current. The slack water directly behind the rock is not the best place to fish a dry fly as fish in this area normally feed in bottom eddies. Your dry fly should be presented to the edge of the current line on either side of the slack water behind the rock. Along this edge is where many trout make their home, holding in the slack water and darting into the current to pick off food.

In Front of Rocks: In front of a rock is another favorite feeding station for trout. The current pushing against the front of a rock is partially deflected upstream, creating a small pocket of slack water immediately in front of the rock. Here trout live without having to fight the force of the current. Your dry fly should be presented to the edge of the first current line on either side of the slack water in front of the rock. It is not profitable to fish in front of all rocks. Rocks that have square or blunt faces which push water upstream, creating slack holding water, are the kinds of rocks you should be looking for.

Rocks Under the Surface: Fish live just behind and just in front of rocks under the surface as they do with rocks showing above the surface. The trick is to be able to learn where sub-surface rocks are located. Occasionally these rocks can be seen just under the water surface. Deeper rocks can usually be detected from the swirling water that submerged rocks create. The swirling currents announcing sub-surface obstructions appear below the obstruction — just how far depends on the swiftness of the current, the shape of the obstruction and its depth in the water. Fish in front and behind submerged rocks just as you would fish surface rocks.

Stream Bars: A stream bar provides an edge between fast and slow currents. The deeper water below the bar moves more slowly than the surface water which sweeps over the bar. The faster water is the cafeteria and the slower is the bedroom, but in the case of bars the effect is reinforced. The photosynthetic processes of algae and plankton taking place within the shallows on the bar is the fundamental base of the aquatic food chain. As a consequence, these bars are the farms which feed the aquatic insects which in turn show up in the trout's diet. Usually bars are clearly visible to the fisherman as an underwater continuation of a shore line structure. Occasionally, however, bars won't be betrayed by shoreline clues. The trained eye quickly observes the surface ripples, much like those revealing sunken rocks, strung out in a linear formation which discloses such a subsurface structure.

When combined with a bend in the stream or any major alteration of the current lines, the bar becomes something more. I call the resulting crescent shaped target zone "the horn of plenty."

A true cornucopia lies in these areas because of the large lateral holding areas and numerous feeding stations. What is attractive to the fish must therefore be equally attractive to the fisherman.

Stream Islands: Treat a stream island as if it were a large rock in the stream. The rules of reading the water that apply to rocks apply the same way to stream islands. As with a rock, the current line is parted by the island. The currents rejoin each other slightly below the tip of the island. Trout hold in the slack water just above where the two current lines come together. Your dry fly should be presented to the first current line on either side of the slack water. Another good holding spot is usually an area 10 to 20 feet downstream from the point where the two current lines collide. The conflicting currents intermeshing with each other create a buffer of relatively slack water where trout hold. The length of this holding area is dependent upon the force of the current.

Tributaries and Stream Temperatures: Where two streams come together a favorite holding area for trout is created. The slack water created between the current lines of the two colliding streams is good trout habitat. Here the trout finds relief from the force of the current and has a cafeteria or current line on either side from which to secure food. Your dry fly should be presented on the edge of the current line on either side of the slack water.

Another productive spot is the area immediately downstream where the two current lines collide. The conflicting currents dissipating each other creates an area of relatively slack water where trout hold. Your dry fly should be presented to the area where the force of the two currents comes together.

In late summer, water temperatures in many streams rise above the comfort zone for trout (above 68 degrees). When this occurs, trout begin searching for cooler more comfortable water. If the temperature of a feeder stream or small tributary is cooler than the main stream, trout will congregate near the point where the feeder stream enters the main river. Here the trout is provided with cooler water from the tributary, but still is in a position to feed in the main river. At this point, it is appropriate to make some general comments about water temperature.

It is important to always take the water temperature of the stream before you begin to fish. Early in the season water temperatures may be so low as to make dry fly fishing all but impossible. When the water temperature is between 35 and 40 degrees trout rarely feed on the surface. In fact, dry fly fishing is rarely productive until the water temperature warms to at least 45 degrees. Between 45 and 68 degrees trout get more active, use more energy and consume more food. This is because trout are cold blooded animals. Warming water temperatures increase the trout's metabolic rate which in turn produces more body activity and more need for food. All things being equal, trout fishing gets better with each degree rise in temperature until the water temperature reaches 66 to 68 degrees. When the water temperature climbs above 68 degrees, the metabolic rate of the trout starts to slow down and feeding declines. This is because warm water does not hold as much oxygen as colder water. As the oxygen level of the water decreases with rising water temperatures, the trout's metabolic rate drops in order to allow the trout to function with less oxygen. This is the time when trout go to rapids and riffles for oxygenated water. When the water temperature reaches 75 to 80 degrees, trout become very sluggish and are very difficult to catch. Most species of trout cannot survive water temperatures above 85 degrees.

Stream water temperature is usually the coldest just at sunrise. Water temperature normally rises during the day reaching its peak temperature approximately one hour later than the peak air temperature. For example, if the high for the day is reached at 2:30 p.m., then the maximum water temperature will usually be reached at 3:30 p.m. Early in the season there is generally little surface activity until late in the afternoon when the water temperature reaches its peak. During the long hot days of mid-summer, the afternoon water temperature on many western waters may be so warm that the trout become sluggish and hard to catch. When this occurs be sure to take the water temperature of each tributary or feeder stream that you encounter while fishing. Many times you will find that the water temperature of entering streams will be considerably lower than the main river. The confluence of the two is often a prime place to fish.

Next to the Bank – First Current Line: Trout often hold near the bank on the edge of the slack water and the first current line. This feeding station is easy to identify. The water right next to the shore typically has little or no current. Slightly out from the slack water a current line can be seen marking the beginning of moving water. The slope of the bank affects the distance from the bank where the first current or feeding line will be found. Flat banks have a side zone of still water before the first current line is reached. Steep banks, on the other hand, normally mean that the first current line will be very close to the shore. At this edge is where you want to present your dry fly. Trout live here because they don't have to fight the current and the nearby current line constantly brings a concentration of insects. A mistake that many fishermen make is that they place their dry fly too far out into the strong current. Trout are not normally found in non-obstructed fast water because they consume too much energy staying in this kind of water in relationship to the food that is available.

Undercut Banks: Undercut banks are usually found at a bend in a stream or on a river with grassy banks. Undercut banks are created by the centrifugal force of the water cutting away at the soft grassy lower bank, thereby creating an underwater pocket into the bank. Your dry fly should be presented to the first current line in front of the undercut bank. Several drifts may be necessary to bring the trout out of its hiding place. The undercut bank offers protection from predators, a good source of food and often slack water — the favorite ingredients for a trout.

Back Eddy: Large trout love the sanctuary of a back eddy. Here they are provided with slack water and a cafeteria line of food right at their front door. Trout normally hold in the collision zone between the eddy's return current and the main flow. Often the feeding station will be marked by a patch of foam which has, like the insects within it, been trapped by the conflicting currents. Very large back eddies become streams within a stream — the fish holding along the shore facing into the current just as they do elsewhere. Any of the current edges inside the pattern of circling water can become a feeding line. Slack water eddies are one of my favorite areas to work a streamer or a Muddler Minnow. Often small fish are attracted to back eddies to get relief from the forces of the current and are fed upon by the large fish holding there for the same reason.

Tail of a Pool: Water slows down in a pool and then speeds up again at the tail of the pool. Current lines get close together at the tail, funneling insects through the pool. Trout hold in the slack water or "V" just above where the current lines rejoin. Trout holding in this position are able to dart into the current on either side of their sanctuary to pick up morsels of food. Your dry fly should be presented to the first current line on either side of the "V."

The key element in water reading is training your eye to detect the edges of current between fast and slack water. You must then interpret these observations and apply the general principles of water reading. Taking the time to sit down and analyze your water will pay off in dividends.

CASTING METHODS DESIGNED TO ELIMINATE DRAG

The late Merton Parks, considered by many as one of the finest western fly fishermen, used to say that there are three important aspects of dry fly fishing to master — presentation, pattern and size. Presentation is the most important. The key to presentation is the elimination of drag.

The conflicting currents found on most swift, rough, mountain streams make a drag-free presentation difficult. Drag occurs whenever the artificial floats either faster or slower than the natural drift of the current. This signals to the trout that the fly is a fake and prevents a strike. Proper casting techniques can greatly reduce drag.

Slack Line Casts: Slack line casts are used in the familiar situation where there is faster water between you and the trout. The trick is being able to cast in such a manner as to throw a series of "S" waves into the line to absorb the speed of the fast current so that your fly has a few feet of natural or drag free float in the slower current.

There are many different methods of performing a slack line cast. Probably the easiest method is to make the back cast in the normal manner and then over-power the forward cast so that the line bounces off the rod tip, falling to the water in a series of "S" waves. The amount of slack can be increased by tilting the plane of the forward cast at about a 10 degree angle away from the water so that in effect the cast is made slightly uphill. When the over-powered line suddenly hits the rod tip, instead of falling straight down to the water, the line will fall backward towards the caster in a series of large "S" waves.

The main difficulty with both of these casting methods is that it is hard to be very accurate while over-powering the operation.

A method of performing a slack line cast that gives better accuracy is the lazy "S" cast. This method is performed by making several false casts over the target in order to gauge the distance to be cast. As the final forward cast passes over the head of the caster the rod is moved rapidly from side to side until the line hits the water. This side to side motion or "quiver" causes a series of "S" waves to form in the line.

Curve Cast to the Right and Left: Curve casts are designed to eliminate drag by placing a portion of the line above the fly to absorb current speed, allowing the imitation a period of time to float drag free.

Curve to the Left: The curve to the left or the positive curve is performed in the following manner. First, tilt the rod so that it is at a 45 degree angle in relationship to the water. Next, make the back cast in the normal manner for the distance to be cast. The forward cast is over-powered so that the line will bounce off the rod tip falling to the water surface in a curve to the left. The degree of the curve is determined by the tilt of the rod. The more the rod is tilted towards the water the more pronounced the curve will become.

Curve to the Right: The curve to the right or the negative curve is made by performing the back cast in the normal manner with full power for the distance to be cast. However, the forward cast is made verly slowly allowing the cast to die before the loop has a chance to straighten out. If you experience the problem of the line straightening out before the line hits the water, try dropping your rod toward the water while executing your forward cast. This will get the line on the water quicker, giving less time for the line to straighten.

Mending the Line: As the line floats downstream, faster currents catch the line putting a belly in the line which causes the artificial to float faster than the speed of the current. This problem can be alleviated by mending the line. This is accomplished in the following manner: First, lower the rod tip so that it is pointed directly at the line on the water's surface. Next, flip the belly of the line upstream with a half turn or twist of the wrist. This will allow the fly to float drag free until the current bellies the line again and the process must be repeated.

IMPORTANT POINTS TO REMEMBER

1. On mayfly streams use attractor patterns with upright wings like the Royal Wulff and Humpy.

2. On caddisfly streams use a downwinged attractor pattern like the Coachman Trude or fore and aft hackle patterns such as the Buzz Hackle and Renegade.

3. On streams that have a significant population of both mayflies and caddisflies use the Humpy.

4. On streams that have a caddisfly and stonefly population use the Coachman Trude.

5. Attractor patterns are best used on rough, broken, swift water when a hatch is not taking place.

6. If you are fishing rough, broken, swift water and are not sure of the predominant insect hatch on the stream, I suggest that you start with a Humpy.

7. When reading the water look for the edges between fast and slack current.

8. Dry fly fishing is rarely productive until stream water temperature reaches 45 degrees. Between 45 and 68 degrees fishing improves.

9. Use "S" casts and mending techniques to help counter the problem of drag.

BUZZ HACKLE

THE Buzz Hackle was first tied in 1928 for Al Lent by E.C. Powell's wife, Myrtle. According to Walton Powell, Lent, a frequently skunked client, wanted a fly which had all the good things on it that worked for his partners. "Some peacock, some tinsel, something red, grey hackle and brown," were the original specifications. Our dressing is taken directly from the original sample provided us by Walton Powell.

When Lent tried the fly he outfished all the members of his party. The Lent Fly, as it was originally christened, became an instant success. Two years later Mr. Lent asked the Powells to rename the fly in honor of his infant son "Buzz" Lent. The Buzz Hackle still has a loyal following along the Sierra foothills.

HOOK:	94840, sizes 8-14.
THREAD:	Black 3/0 mono-cord.
TAIL:	Red hackle fibers, tail tied down over the bend of the hook.
BODY:	Rear segment — silver tinsel. Center segment — peacock herl. Front segment — gold tinsel.
RIB:	Rear tinsel segment palmered with grizzly one hook size small. Forward tinsel segment palmered with furnace hackle normal size.

1. Make a tail from heavy stiff red hackle fibers and secure it to the hook. Continue to wind the thread around the bend of the hook so as to bring the tail into an acute slant relative to the hook shank.

2. Tie on the silver tinsel. Take a few turns with the tinsel, just enough to put the tinsel back to the bend of the hook where the feather is to be tied in. Select your ribbing feather and tie it in with the curve or dull side facing you. Continue to wind your thread over the butt of the ribbing feather and the tail butts.

3. Wind the tinsel body, making sure to keep the turns very tight and close together. Tie the tinsel off with two turns of thread. Wind the ribbing feather with open turns. Trim the ribbing feather and attach a single strand of peacock herl to the hook to make the center peacock body segment.

4. Wind a peacock collar in the center of the fly and tie off the peacock.

5. Select a brown hackle for the forward hackle segment. Tie in the hackle with the curve or dull side facing you. Wind the tinsel over this forward body segment and tie it off.

6. Wind the forward hackle segment. Shape the head, whip finish, and lacquer.

RENEGADE

STONEFLIES AND TERRESTRIALS

PARKS' SALMONFLY

BUCKTAIL CADDIS

BIRD'S STONEFLY

BLACK ANT

JOE'S HOPPER

ROUGH WATER ATTRACTOR FLIES

BUZZ HACKLE

RENEGADE

ADAMS IRRESISTIBLE

HUMPY

ROYAL WULFF

COACHMAN TRUDE

CADDISFLY IMITATIONS

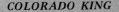

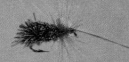

COLORADO KING

KING'S RIVER CADDIS

HENRYVILLE SPECIAL

GODDARD CADDIS

MAYFLY IMITATIONS

ADAMS   GRAY WULFF   LIGHT CAHILL

LIGHT HENDRICKSON   HAIRWING VARIANT   NO-COLOR PARACHUTE

CHARCOAL QUILL   QUILL GORDON   MOSQUITO   POLY-WING SPINNER

THE BASTARD (Midge)   NO-COLOR SIDEWINDER   PARKS-WILSON

THE Renegade is the best known of a large family of fore and aft tied flies. In most of the country these flies are usually fished as wets, but they have proven to be very effective dries in streams with good caddis populations, particularly in the Colorado-New Mexico area.

The Renegade itself is not clearly imitative of any insect. Peacock seems to be able to get into a fish's head and twist it so that it sees what it wants to see. The fore and aft style has been used very successfully to represent caddisflies.

Several variations of the Renegade are nearly as important. When tied with grizzly hackle in back and brown in front it becomes the well known Warden's Worry. The use of grizzly for both the fore and aft hackles produces the fly known as the Gray Ugly.

HOOK:	94840, sizes 10-16.
THREAD:	Black mono-cord.
TIP:	Flat gold tinsel or tinsel thread.
REAR HACKLE:	Brown neck hackle — small for the hook.
BODY:	Peacock herl.
FRONT HACKLE:	White neck hackle.

1. Tie in a few inches of fine mylar or flat gold tinsel. In attaching this tinsel be very careful to get it tight. Place a small amount of head cement on the thread platform prepared for the tinsel and wind the tinsel into place in the cement.

2. Select a brown neck hackle. Secure the hackle to the hook with a series of close turns, making a platform for the hackle feather. Those turns need to be close to maintain a smooth base for the hackle. Wind the hackle feather. Secure the hackle with two turns of the thread.

3. Select a strand of peacock herl and tie it into the fly right up to the brown hackle. Wind the peacock with close turns. Wind the peacock herl back over itself then forward again, building up the body.

4. Select one white neck hackle. Wind the white hackle at the front of the fly, again being careful to make fairly close turns to build up the front hackle. Tie it off with two turns of thread. Shape the head, whip finish, and lacquer.

ADAMS IRRESISTIBLE

THIS fly is one member of a large family tied primarily to combat the tendency of conventional patterns to sink in rough water. William Blades in his *Fishing Flies and Fly Tying* even lists an Irresistible nymph which seems like something of a contradiction. The Irresistible offers a generalized mayfly silhouette best employed on rough water.

The Adams Irresistible is sometimes called the Rat Faced McDougal, but this fly, tied by Harry Darbee, has light ginger hackle rather than the brown and grizzly mix of the Adams. The Irresistible itself is tied with bucktail wings and blue dun hackle, which gives it an appearance very like the Gray Wulff. The two flies are fairly interchangeable, though the Irresistible floats better on very rough water. Numerous other variations can be produced by changing the color of the spun body hair. Some common examples are the Black, Brown, White and Yellow Irresistibles. Bob Quigley, a well known tier located on California's Fall River, uses an Irresistible with a light olive body when fish are feeding on the Western Green Drake.

HOOK:	94840, Sizes 8-14.
THREAD:	Size A mono-cord, black.
TAIL:	Brown bucktail.
BODY:	Clipped deer body hair.
WING:	Grizzly hackle points.
HACKLE:	One brown and one grizzly neck hackle.

1. Cut some hair from the brown base of the bucktail. Attach the tail to the hook with four turns of the thread and trim the butt of the tail at a slant. Place Duco into the butt of the tail and with close, even turns secure the tail.

2. Cut some hair from the deer hide. The most important thing in spinning a hair body like this is to be sure you get all the underfur out of the hair. The underfur will not spin worth a darn. Slide the hair around the hook.

3. Hold the hair and wrap a loose loop of thread around it.

4. Slowly pull this loop tight to spin the hair into a ruff around the hook. Use a second turn of the thread in front of the hair. Place three turns of the thread against the hair to pack it together.

5. Repeat Steps 2 through 4 until the body is full.

6. The body ends at the standard position halfway between the eye and the bend of the hook. Whip finish and cut off the excess thread. (I usually find it more efficient to make all the bodies I need before tying the rest of the fly on any of them.)

7. Remove the fly from the vise and trim the hair to shape.

8. The final body shape must be a smoothly tapering cylinder cut close enough to the hook to clear the gape.

9. Replace the hook in the vise and secure the tying thread to the fly. Select a pair of grizzly hackle points for the wings. Attach the wings to the hook, erecting and dividing them as above.

10. Select one brown and one grizzly hackle. Wind the hackles one at a time, both behind and ahead of the wing. Shape the head, whip finish and seal the head with cement.

HUMPY

THE original fly of this numerous clan was the Horner Deer Hair, tied by the late Jack Horner of San Francisco. The dressing given below is the most common of the variations. You may also find the fly called the Crazy Goof, Tom Thumb or Goofus Bug. Almost any combination of thread color, body hair color and hackle can be used effectively.

My style results in a fairly slim bodied fly. Many authorities, such as Andre Puyans, prefer a very full bodied dressing. There are two ways to achieve this effect, the simplest being to use more hair. However, there is a practical limit to how much hair can be securely handled. The Humpy is an excellent rough water fly representing caddisflies, mayflies, stoneflies and grasshoppers with about equal credibility.

HOOK:	94840, sizes 8-16.
THREAD:	Yellow 3/0 mono-cord.
TAIL:	Dark deer body hair — not too coarse.
BODY:	Dark deer body hair over thread underbody.
WING:	Dark deer body hair (the wing and body hair are the same segment of hair).
HACKLE:	Mixed brown and grizzly hackles.

1. From the hide of a mule deer, trim a small bundle of hair for the tail. Attach the tail with four turns of the thread and trim the butts of the tail.

2. Trim a second bundle of hair from the hide of the mule deer. This should be approximately twice as much hair as would be required for the tail. (It is quite important here to get the hair well aligned.) The hair should be equal in length to the overall distance from the eye to the tip of the tail.

3. Attach with four turns of thread. Hold the wing and back material so that it doesn't slip. Trim the butts with a slant facing forward. Fill the butts of the wing and tail with cement.

4. Secure both sets of hair with fairly loose open turns to capture the trimmed butts of hair on the first pass. Then go over them and make everything tight. Trim off any hairs that are sticking out.

5. Use a little lacquer on the top of the body to help seal it. Pull the wing and back material over.

6. Attach the wing with four turns of tying thread to secure the hair at the wing position.

7. Erect and divide the wings as usual for hair flies. Placing several turns of the thread against the butt of the wing will hold it erect. Divide the wings with the bodkin, then put figure 8's between the wings.

8. Prepare one brown and one grizzly hackle for the hackle of the fly. Wind the hackles one at a time with a couple of turns behind the wing and finishing in front of the wing. Shape the head, whip finish, and cement.

ROYAL WULFF

LEE Wulff worked out the first of the Wulff patterns in 1929 and subsequently collaborated with Montana's Dan Bailey on the creation of other members of the family. The Royal Wulff, an obvious derivation from the venerable Coachman tradition, is the best known member of this group. The essence of a rough water attractor, the Royal Wulff is the most visible of divided wing flies on broken water. The basic silhouette of the Wulff is that of the mayfly, but rough water breaks up color and shape patterns, giving the fish an opportunity to mistake the fly for a lot of things.

The name Wulff is becoming somewhat generic in the sense that it means an upright, divided hair wing dry fly. Used without other clarification however, it almost invariably means a Royal Wulff. Some tiers use moose body hair or peccary for the tail, which is a minor change. When tied with white calf tail for the tail as well as the wings the fly is frequently called the Hairwing Royal Coachman. Most of the other variations that have been tried with the Royal Coachman could also be applied to the Wulff.

56

HOOK:	94840, sizes 8-16.
THREAD:	Black mono-cord 3/0.
TAIL:	Brown bucktail.
BODY:	Peacock herl with red floss center segment.
WING:	White calf tail, erected and divided.
HACKLE:	Brown saddle hackles.

1. Secure the tail material to the hook with four turns of the tying thread.

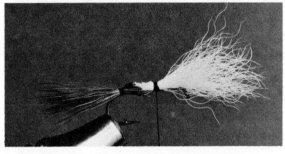

2. Clip calf tail from the stem. Judge the wing length, checking the wing against the length of the hook. The wing should extend from the eye to the bend of the hook.

3. Attach a strand of peacock for the rearmost peacock segment of the body. Wind this peacock segment forward to the position even with the point of the hook.

4. Attach the red floss and wind two turns for the center body segment.

5. Wind the second peacock body segment.

6. Erect the wings by pulling the wing material back towards the bend of the hook. Make four turns of thread against the base of the wing. Divide the wings with figure eights. Wrap a three-turn "collar" (see page 25 for complete instructions) around each wing base. Seal with cement.

 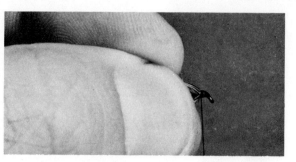

7. Secure the hackles to the fly behind the wings. Wind the hackles one at a time, starting with two turns behind the wing. Bring the hackles in front of the wing and take several more turns.

8. Guarding the hackles between thumb and first two fingers of the left hand, shape the head, whip finish, and cement.

COACHMAN TRUDE

THE original fly of the Trude series was apparently created as a jest by Carter Harrison in 1903 on the Trude Ranch in Idaho. Fuzz of rug and hair of dog produced a fly too good to remain a joke. The name "Trude," originally applied by Harrison in honor of his host, has since become a generic term usually designating a fly using a down calf-tail wing.

The first Trudes were wet flies essentially similar to the present Squirrel Tail patterns. Our Coachman variation and its companion the Royal Trude are obvious derivations applying the hair-wing idea to the standard patterns. The general concept of the Trude has been applied to many color combinations. Today there are Trudes of almost every conceivable shade.

The beauty of the Trude is that while it looks like nothing in particular, except possibly a caddis-fly, the fish have the habit of turning it into anything they want it to be. It is an excellent caddis imitation on broken water and can readily be taken by fish as a stonefly, or even a mayfly. I have had excellent success with it in a size 16 when the fish are working the snow fly hatch. Only the Royal Wulff matches the Trude as a rough water attractor.

HOOK:	94840, sizes 10-18.
THREAD:	Black mono-cord.
TAIL:	Golden Pheasant tippet.
BODY:	Peacock herl.
WING:	White calf tail.
HACKLE:	Brown neck hackle.

1. Trim several fibers from a Golden Pheasant tippet for the tail, being careful to keep the tips aligned. Attach the tail to the hook with four turns of the thread.

2. Tie in a peacock herl for the body. (If you are tying large Trudes, you will probably need to use two peacock herls.) Wind the peacock herl with fairly close turns.

3. Trim some hair from the calf tail and prepare a wing. The wing position is a point halfway between the point on the hook and the eye. Secure the wing to the hook.

4. Select and prepare two neck hackles. Attach the hackle with three turns of the thread. Wind the hackles as usual, one at a time, securing each hackle with two turns of thread. Use the second hackle to fill in any spaces between the turns of the first hackle. Shape the head, whip finish, and cement.

Chapter V
Fishing and Tying
Caddisfly Imitations

UNTIL recently, the dry fly caddis imitation has not enjoyed very much popularity for two important reasons. First, many fishermen have a difficult time recognizing that a caddis hatch is taking place, even though in many western rivers caddisfly hatches take place almost daily. This is because the adult caddisfly (order *Trichoptera*) does not float along in the surface film drying its wings like the mayfly. The adult caddisfly takes to the air almost immediately upon emerging through the surface. Caddisflies are seldom, if ever, seen drifting on the surface film. Therefore, the angler that is accustomed to fishing an insect hatch signaled by flies drifting on the surface will often completely miss the caddis hatch. Secondly, even if the fisherman is aware that some kind of hatch is taking place, he may not be familiar with the appearance of the winged adult caddisfly. Therefore, he will not carry dry fly patterns to represent this insect.

In order to determine if a caddisfly hatch is taking place the fisherman must make two important observations. First, the manner of the rise form must be observed. Rises that are splashy are often indicative of trout chasing fast moving caddis pupae to the surface. Many times the caddis pupa is too fast for the trout and it will escape to the surface and fly away. A close observation of the rise ring will sometimes detect the missed caddisfly escaping. During a caddisfly hatch on flat smooth water a small "V" shaped wake will often be seen on the surface as trout chase caddis pupae just under the surface.

The observation of trout jumping completely out of the water is an almost certain sign that trout are chasing caddis pupae. "Causeless" rise rings, which are the result of caddisflies emerging through the surface film, is another clue to their activity.

The observation of caddis cases on submerged stream rocks is a sure sign that caddisflies are present. This, of course, doesn't mean that a hatch is in progress, only that hatches at certain times do take place. The observation of caddisflies in flight or on nearby stream bushes is indicative of a caddis hatch in progress.

For those fishermen who have difficulty identifying a caddisfly, the following chart comparing the characteristics of a caddisfly, mayfly and stonefly will be helpful.

Wings:

Caddisfly — has two sets of hairy wings of nearly equal length. The wing length is nearly one-third longer than the body. The two sets of hairy wings, when at rest, fold back on top of each other in an inverted "V" or tent-like manner. The adult caddisfly looks much like a moth while in flight. It also appears much larger in flight than its true size. Caddisflies have a tendency to look lighter in color while in flight than their actual color.

Mayfly — Most mayfly species have two large wings and two small wings. Both sets of wings stand upright and slant backward at about a 45-degree angle. The wings of mayflies are about the same length as their bodies.

Stonefly — The stonefly has two sets of wings of nearly equal length. Like the caddisfly its wings are approximately one-third longer than its body. The two sets of wings fold back flat over the body and are not tent-shaped like the wings of a caddisfly.

Tail:
Caddisfly — Has no tail.
Mayfly — Has two and sometimes three long thin tails. Tail length may be as long as the body.
Stonefly — Has two tails. Tail length is about two-thirds the length of the body.
Antennae:
Caddisfly — Normally has two very long antennae. Most species have antennae which are twice as long as their bodies.
Mayfly — Has two very short antennae that are barely noticeable.
Stonefly — Has two antennae about the same length as their tail.

A knowledge of the caddisfly's life cycle is helpful in understanding the rationale behind the various techniques of fishing the caddisfly. The life cycle of the caddisfly starts with:

Egg: The caddis egg hatches in a few weeks into a small caterpillar or worm-like entity known as a larva.

Larva: During this stage most species of caddisflies go to work building a case or protective shell, usually out of tiny pieces of gravel or wood. Some species of caddisflies weave tiny food catching nets and attach them to their cases. The case serves as camouflage and as an environment for further development. Some important western caddis genera like *Rhyacophila* and *Hydropsyche*, known as free swimmers, do not build cases. However, these genera at pupation do form a cocoon like envelope.

Pupa: During this stage the cased caddis close off the open end of their cases. In this closed off environment, legs, antennae and wings are developed. The non-case makers form a cocoon like shell for protection during this stage. When the caddisfly is fully developed, the pupa breaks open the protective shell surrounding it and with the help of trapped gas bubbles rapidly ascends to the surface, where it emerges as an adult. During this period trout chase the ascending pupa to the surface and produce the splashy rises and wakes discussed earlier.

Adult: This is the stage which the angler is attempting to imitate with dry flies. The caddis is now fully formed. During the adult period the female caddisfly lays its eggs, which is called ovipositing. Two forms of ovipositing are of interest to the fisherman. One form of ovipositing consists of the female caddis entering the water, laying its eggs on a sub-surface structure and re-emerging. Normally this takes place by the egg laden female caddisfly landing on a rock protruding above the surface of the stream. Slowly the insect crawls down the rock into the water to lay its eggs. During this underwater adventure the caddisfly is very vulnerable to the trout. The method of caddis fishing known as the downstream twitch dive is designed to imitate the caddis ovipositing under water in this fashion. The other form of ovipositing consists of the female caddis fluttering over the surface of the water and occasionally dipping its abdomen into the water thereby depositing the eggs. The method of caddis fishing known as the downstream flutter cast is designed to imitate the caddis while ovipositing in this manner.

Before starting to fish a caddis imitation, it is very important to collect a sample of the natural. Sometimes this is difficult to do as the flight of the caddis is very erratic. A larger net is normally required than that needed to capture a mayfly. It may take awhile to catch specimens, but it is important. If you find that you are having real difficulties attempting to capture a caddis with a net, look on the shady side of the leaves of streamside bushes for resting caddis. You will probably discover after collecting a sample that the natural is much smaller than it looked in flight. Most caddisflies are smaller than one-half inch. Those fishermen who begin fishing without collecting a sample normally end up using a fly that is at least two sizes larger than the natural.

Caddisflies appear lighter in color in flight than they actually are. The captured insects will always be a dull color due to the microscopic strands of hair that cover their wings. The most common body colors are shades of brown and gray. Avoid using bright colors to imitate this insect. Caddisflies are not imitated well by the typical dry fly imitation tied with upright wings. This insect is downwinged and should be imitated with a representative downwing dry fly.

Caddisflies have long antennae. Most of the standard caddis patterns tied in this chapter can be improved by adding antennae. Moose hair, peccary or dyed brown monofilament works well for this purpose. Strength is given to this material by varnishing each strand of the antennae. Remember to make the antennae as long as the body length.

CADDISFLY FISHING TECHNIQUES

The trick to successfully fishing caddisfly imitations is learning to impart to your fly the behavior of the adult caddis. Caddisflies skip, flutter and bounce on the water's surface. Rarely does this insect sit motionless on the surface like most mayflies. The fishing techniques set out below are designed to allow the fisherman to mimic the behavior of the adult caddisfly.

Downstream Flutter Cast: This method is designed to represent the adult caddis skipping and fluttering on the surface, as well as the female caddis fluttering briefly on the water surface during ovipositing. The flutter cast is accomplished by making a short cast downstream and across. In order to produce a drag free float, point the rod tip toward the water at about a 45 degree angle and shake the rod tip so that line will feed out fast enough to allow the fly to float with the current drag free. At frequent intervals as the fly floats downstream, twitch it slightly upstream to create a fluttering or skipping effect. The twitch is accomplished by lifting the rod tip so that it pulls against the fly line causing the caddis imitation to make a slight upstream movement. Most fishermen tend to overdo this. An upstream twitch of one-half to one inch is all that is needed.

This method, although it has been around for a long time, was recently popularized by Leonard Wright in his book *Fishing the Dry Fly as a Living Insect.* Wright calls this upstream movement "the sudden inch." This method works best if the slight twitch is done just in front of a rising fish. Frequently, the twitching motion will cause a reluctant trout to strike with abandonment. The Goddard Caddis, originated by John Goddard of England, is particularly suited for the flutter method. The deer hair body construction makes this fly almost impossible to sink by even the most enthusiastic twitch. Caddis imitations like the Henryville Special, Colorado King, King's River Caddis and Bucktail Caddis are also effective when fished in this manner.

The Downstream Twitch Dive: Same as the downstream flutter cast, but at the end of the cast let the current take the dry fly slightly beneath the surface. As the fly dips below the surface, begin feeding line so that the fly floats drag free under the water. At frequent intervals slightly twitch the fly upstream. As with the downstream flutter cast, only a one-half to one inch forward movement is needed. This method is suggestive of the adult female caddis struggling to reach the surface after ovipositing under water. This method works extremely well during July and August on the Yellowstone River between Gardiner and Livingston, Montana. The King's River Caddis is very effective for this purpose. I have found that if a small ball of green thread or fur, suggestive of an egg sack, is tied just under the tail of the King's River Caddis that the number of strikes increases dramatically.

The Conventional Dead Drift Cast: Female caddisflies oviposit by dipping their abdomens into the water. When their egg laying is completed they often float exhausted and motionless on the surface of the water. The traditional upstream dead-drift cast imparts to the dry fly the behavior of the exhausted female caddisfly. The dead drift method also works well when both caddisflies and small stoneflies are hatching at the same time. The downwing character of caddisfly imitations serves to represent both the downwing caddisfly and the downwing stonefly. The King's River Caddis works particularly well in representing both the adult caddisfly and small stoneflies.

No discussion of fishing caddisfly imitations would be complete without a word about the great western *Dicosmoecus* hatch. These large (hook sizes 6 to 8), darkish-orange caddisflies emerge in late September and October on many Pacific Coast streams. The hatch lasts two to three weeks depending on the stream and water conditions. When this hatch is on, trout will feed almost exclusively on this huge fly. On many western rivers the *Dicosmoecus* caddisfly hatch rivals the salmonfly hatch. In California, the *Dicosmoecus* hatch hits the upper Sacramento River about the first week in October. During this period the upper Sacramento is alive with big fish.

The Bucktail Caddis, tied with a dull orange underbody works well to match this hatch. The Parks' Salmonfly, tied on a size 8 hook, also works well for this purpose.

Those fishermen who are interested in learning to fish all phases of the caddis hatch, not just the dry fly phase presented here, are strongly recommended to read Larry Solomon's and Eric Leiser's book entitled *The Caddis and the Angler.*

IMPORTANT POINTS TO REMEMBER

    1. Many anglers are not aware that a caddis hatch is taking place for two reasons.
        a. Caddisflies are seldom seen drifting on the surface film.
        b. Many fishermen are not familiar with the appearance of a caddisfly and therefore carry no patterns to represent this insect.
    2. Splashy rises, fish jumping completely out of the water, and "causeless rises" are often indicative of a caddis hatch.
    3. Observation of caddisflies in flight or on bushes near the stream signals a caddis hatch.
    4. Caddisflies have two sets of wings that fold back, when at rest in an inverted "V." They have no tails but have two long antennae.
    5. Before starting to fish, always collect a sample. Caddisflies look much larger and lighter in color in flight than they actually are.
    6. Caddisflies are downwinged insects and should be imitated in this manner. Avoid using bright colors. The most common body colors are brown and gray.
    7. When caddisflies are observed fluttering and bouncing around on the surface, the downstream flutter cast works best. The traditional upstream dead-drift presentation is effective during the few times when caddisflies float motionless on the surface.
    8. The downstream twitch dive represents the adult female caddis ovipositing under water.

COLORADO KING

GEORGE Bodmer, the creator of the Colorado King, writes: "I developed the pattern as an attractor, combining a recent run of good success with a Montana Bucktail with the advantages of the splayed tail fibers that were so successful on the No-Hackle flies. . . ." He goes on to say that after an initial period of experimentation he settled on the basic variations now used.

The Dark Colorado King given below is easily modified to meet other color requirements. The Light Colorado King uses yellow fur and light deer hair while the Brown Colorado King uses brown fur and brown hackle. It may pay to try additional color combinations as Bodmer believes that the fly can function as an attractor, a mayfly or a caddis.

63

HOOK:	94840, sizes 10-16.
THREAD:	Black 3/0 mono-cord.
TAIL:	Two peccary* fibers spread.
BODY:	Dubbed muskrat.
RIB:	Grizzly palmered hackle.
WING:	Deer body hair tied short so as to extend only a little past the bend of the hook.

*Peccary is body hair from the wild pig.

1. Make a dubbing loop as described in the techniques section. Pull a small strand of fur from the fur ball to make the dubbing for the tail hump. Spin the dubbing and make one turn of the finished yarn.

2. Select two peccary fibers and clip them from the hide. Attach them on each side of the hook so that they are spread around the tail hump. Secure them with two turns of the thread.

3. Select a feather two sizes smaller than usual for the rib. Before attaching it to the hook strip all the barbules off one side.

4. Prepare a normal strand of fur for the remainder of the dubbed body. Dub the fur body forward to the wing position.

5. Using open turns wind the ribbing feather forward and secure it with two turns of the thread.

6. Clip a group of hairs from the deer hide. The wing length should be short, extending only to the bend of the hook. Attach the wing with four turns of the thread. Form the head, whip finish, and lacquer.

KING'S RIVER CADDIS

ORIGINALLY tied by the late "Buz" Buszek of Visalia, California, for the King's River, this
fly has become a standard caddis imitation throughout the West. I believe it will also successfully represent stoneflies when tied in appropriate sizes and colors.

This fly is adaptable to a wide range of colors. I use orange yarn for the body but other materials could easily be used. Using gray duck wing quill establishes another color tone. Either of
these wings could present a tying problem in small sizes. That part of the wing quill close to the
stem is quite thick and won't roll over a small hook. This problem is readily solved by moving
the attachment point toward the tip of the quill segment.

HOOK:	94840, sizes 6-18.
THREAD:	Black mono-cord.
BODY:	Orange yarn.
RIB:	Brown hackle tied palmer and clipped.
WING:	Rolled mottled turkey.
HACKLE:	Brown neck hackle.

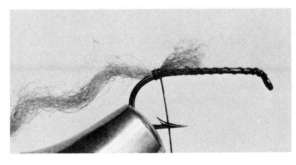

1. Unravel a piece of orange yarn into its
separate strands and attach one strand to
the hook with four turns of thread.

2. Select a large brown neck hackle to be
used for the ribbing feather. Carefully
wind the thread over the entire butt of the
feather and yarn with close turns. Wind
the body with the orange yarn, being very
careful to get an extremely tight turn behind the ribbing feather.

3. Now wind the ribbing feather, making one complete turn at the butt followed by open turns forward over the orange yarn underbody.

4. Trim the palmered rib quite close to the hook.

5. Roll the turkey wing quill over the hook, with the base of the quill segment facing the rear of the hook. Attach the wing with four turns of the thread. Trim the butt of the wing extending past the eye of the hook with a slant facing forward.

6. Wind the hackles one at a time. Shape the head, whip finish, and cement.

HENRYVILLE SPECIAL

POSSIBLY derived from English roots, the Henryville Special was originally a Pennsylvania pattern. Taking its name from the Henryville area in the Poconos Mountains, this pattern proved very successful during the '20's and '30's. The Henryville's design concept makes it one of the best imitations of the adult caddis available. Recent increased attention to caddisflies has resurrected this standby and made it the jumping off point for many local variations.

The fly can be varied to suit particular needs. The body and wing materials can be varied as can

66

the color of the palmer rib. While the color tones of the natural caddisflies are dull, earthy tones, there is still a wide range of possibilities in any given area. The most used pattern in my area, for instance, uses brown hackle for the palmer over a black thread underbody.

HOOK:	94840, sizes 12-18.
THREAD:	Black 3/0 mono-cord.
BODY:	Olive sparkle yarn (or substitute floss).
RIB:	Grizzly hackle palmer.
UNDERWING:	Woodduck or mallard dyed woodduck.
WING:	Slate duck wing quill.
HACKLE:	Sparse brown hackle.

1. Attach the body yarn with three turns of thread, following it with the ribbing feather tied in by its point. Individual hackle barbules tend to become shorter toward the point of the feather so that tying a feather by its tip insures that the longest barbules will be at the front of the fly.

2. Trim any of the yarn and hackle point that extends beyond the wing position before securing these butts. Wind the body yarn with tight turns. Wind the ribbing feather with open turns.

3. Trim short only those barbules of the rib which are on the top of the body, leaving a channel in the ribbing.

4. Strip a small group of fibers from the flank feather for the underwing. Attach the underwing with four turns of thread so that the wing extends beyond the bend of the hook.

5. Trim the wings from a pair of gray duck wing quills. This overwing extends only to the bend of the hook and should be attached on the sides of the hook. Keep the tips of the wings aligned while tying them on.

6. Select a single hackle feather of normal size for the hook. Attach the hackle and wind on two turns. Shape the head, whip finish, and cement.

GODDARD CADDIS

WE were first informed of the Goddard Caddis by Andre Puyans of Creative Sports in Walnut Creek, California. Andy told us that he had gotten the pattern from John Goddard, an English flyfisher of some reknown. A recent import, Goddard's Caddis is bound to increase in popularity due to its extreme floatability. It's difficult to sink, even under a waterfall.

As more experience is gained with the fly I fully expect it to become the leading member of a large family of variations. It is a design idea readily adaptable to many circumstances. Almost any set of color tones exhibited by natural caddisflies can be reproduced by using one or more colors of hair for the body and an appropriate hackle. The Pantone pen no-color concept employed with mayfly patterns could also be used with this fly.

HOOK:	94840, sizes 8-14.
THREAD:	Black 3/0 mono-cord.
TAIL:	None.
BODY:	Spun deer hair dyed brown and trimmed to caddis shape.
WING:	None.
HACKLE:	Brown neck hackle.
ANTENNAE:	Dyed monofilament (or hackle stems).

1. Trim dyed deer hair from the hide and prepare it by knocking out the underfur. Work the hair around the hook and make a loose turn of thread over it. Then pull the loop tight to spin out the hair.

2. Repeat this step as required. Tie off the thread with a whip finish. Remove the fly from the vise and trim the hair into the body shape. Create the typical caddis tent shape. Once the body is shaped, return the fly to the vise.

3. Attach the monofilament antennae.

4. Select two brown hackles one size smaller than normal. Wind the hackles one at a time and tie each off with two turns of thread. Trim the hackle points and shape the head. Whip finish and lacquer the head.

69

Chapter VI

Fishing and Tying
Mayfly Imitations

MAYFLIES on many western streams and rivers make up the largest percentage of the diet of trout. They have been nicknamed mayflies because in most places in the Northern Hemisphere their hatch begins in may. In tropical climates mayflies hatch all year long.

In the United States there are over 500 species of mayflies. About 120 species have a significant enough hatch to be important to trout. There are over 200 dry fly patterns designed to imitate this insect. It would take a life-time to learn the latin names and characteristics of all the mayfly species.

Mayflies (order *Ephemeroptera*) have upright wings that slant back from their bodies at about a 45 degree angle. Most species have two pairs of wings — the front pair normally being three times as long as the hind pair. A few species have only one pair of upright wings. Overall wing length is usually a little longer than body length. Mayflies have two or three long thin tails and two short antennae. Mayflies always fly in the vertical position with their tails hanging below them. When drifting in the current mayflies are best described as looking like tiny sailboats.

Mayflies have an interesting life cycle: egg, nymph, dun (subimago) and spinner (imago).

Egg: Incubation period can last anywhere from a few weeks to as long as a year. During the winter months on many western rivers, mayfly eggs go into a kind of hibernation known technically as an impasse. When the water warms in the spring the gestation process resumes until the eggs hatch. The eggs of most species are very small, about the same size as a single knot tied with 6X tippet material. In fact, sometimes trout will strike at leader knots mistaking them for mayfly eggs floating in the current. During the incubation period, legs, tail and antennae are developed. Eggs hatch into an aquatic life form called a nymph.

Nymph: About 99% of the mayflies' existence is spent in the nymphal stage. During this stage as many as 30 molts or shedding of the outer skin takes place. Gills and wing cases are developed. When the nymph is fully developed it struggles to the surface, sheds its nymphal skin or shuck and becomes a winged insect called a dun.

Dun: After emergence most species of mayflies (or duns as they are now called), drift along on the surface of the water drying their wings in preparation to fly away. During this period they are very vulnerable to trout. When the drying process is completed, normally in a matter of a few seconds, the mayfly flies to a nearby bush or tree. It is here that their sexual organs expand, causing the final molt or shedding of their skin to take place. The mayfly is now known as a spinner. Duns invariably fly away from the stream. Spinners always fly toward the stream or other water suitable for egg laying.

Spinner: After the final molt is completed the mayfly takes on a slightly different appearance. The wings of the spinner become almost transparent and the tail length almost doubles. Most spinners now have slightly larger bodies because of the growth of their sexual organs. During this period mating occurs in flight by the male mayfly touching his genitalia to a small duct opening on the abdomen of the female. After fertilization takes place the female deposits her eggs into the stream or any nearby water. Mayflies will even lay their eggs on wet pavement or in rain puddles. Eggs laid in water without a good oxygen supply will quickly die. Shortly after mating is completed both male and female die. Dead spinners are often seen drifting downstream with their wings extending straight out from their body.

It is possible to make some generalizations about the coloration, size, characteristics and hatch times of Western mayflies. I have labeled these generalizations as "Western Mayfly Rules." The more you learn about streamside entomology and the specific kinds of mayflies and other insects that hatch in your area, the better fly fisherman you will become.

WESTERN MAYFLY RULES

1. Mayflies tend to be darker in coloration in spring and fall than they are in the summer.
2. Mayfly body coloration is closely matched by one of the following colors: brown, olive, gray, yellow, tan or cream.
3. There is a correlation between mayfly body and wing coloration. If a particular mayfly has a dark colored body (brown, olive or gray), then wing color will usually be some shade of dark gray. (One exception is the *Tricorythodes*.) Mayflies with yellow, tan or cream bodies are best matched by light gray wings.
4. On dark cloudy days, mayfly imitations that are colored slightly darker than the natural work best. On bright sunny days, especially when the sun is directly overhead, imitations that are colored slightly lighter than the natural work best.
5. Mayfly imitations, tied on hook sizes 14 to 20, will match 95% of the mayfly hatches (an exception is the Western Green Drake hatch).
6. Most hatches in the spring and fall take place in the afternoon when the weather is warmest.
7. Mayfly hatches in the summer may take place at any time of the day. However, hatches are most likely to take place early in the morning or late in the evening.
8. Most mayfly hatches begin in the shallow water and gradually move out to deeper water.
9. Mayfly hatches usually start on the side of the stream or river that gets the most sunlight.
10. Spinners usually fall to the surface in the evening. A few species of mayflies have a mid-morning spinner fall. Spinners are best imitated by dry flies tied in the full spent-wing position.
11. On streams that are clear, slow-moving and have an unbroken surface, Paraduns, No Hackle mayfly imitations or Parachute style flies work best.
12. On fast-moving, rough-water streams, the more impressionistic mayfly imitations like the Adams, House & Lot, Cahill, Quill Gordon and Gray Wulff work best. On this kind of water attractor patterns like the Royal Wulff and Humpy also work well.

RULES OF HATCH MATCHING

From an examination of the basic rules, it is apparent that to be able to match most hatches that you might encounter, you should carry in your fly box either Paradun or No Hackle imitations in the following body/wing coloration: 1) brown/dark gray, 2) olive/dark gray, 3) gray/dark gray, 4) yellow/light gray, 5) tan/light gray, and 6) cream/light gray.

I prefer Paraduns over the No Hackle because in my experience, Paraduns float better, are easier to see and the single wing of this fly presents a more realistic mayfly wing silhouette than the dual winged No Hackle.

No matter which pattern you choose, these flies should be tied in hooks sizes 14 to 20. In addition, the impressionistic mayfly patterns (Adams, House & Lot, Cahill, Quill Gordon and Gray Wulff) should also be included in your selection in hooks sizes 14 to 20, along with a spent-wing spinner pattern in the same hook sizes. We have found that this fly selection will match about 95% of the important mayfly hatches that take place in the West.

The number of patterns listed does not seem like many until you actually add them up. The six Paradun or No Hackle imitations (whichever you prefer) tied on hook sizes 14 to 20 translate into the need to carry 24 selections. The five impressionistic patterns when tied on the same hook sizes, add another 20 patterns. The spinner imitation tied in hook sizes 14 to 20 adds another four patterns. The total number of flies necessary to match most mayfly hatches now amounts to a staggering total of 48. There are at least three ways to cut down on the number needed to match the hatch.

First: Tie the Paradun or No Hackle imitations with a white dubbed body of rabbit fur or white yarn. In the case of the No Hackle make the wings light gray. If tying Paraduns, make the wing loop with white bucktail. Then take with you to the stream six Pantone marking pens. (These pens can be purchased at most fly and hobby shops.) The pens should be purchased in the following colors: brown, olive, tan, gray, cream and yellow. These pens are permanent and water proof. Simply color the body and wings of your imitations to match the color of the natural that is hatching on any particular day. This method is very effective and it allows you to cut down on over 20 of the patterns that are needed for matching the hatch. Remember on dark cloudy days, to give the fly more visibility, color your imitation slightly darker than the natural and on bright sunny days color the imitation slightly lighter than the natural.

Second: If you are familiar with the particular genus and species of mayflies that hatch in your area you will not need to carry the large assortment of imitations that is needed when you fish the water blind. During the early season (April and May) the hatch that you will most likely encounter on a western stream or river is the Blue Winged Olive (*Baetis*) hatch. Typical body color is dark olive to almost a gray. Wing color is medium gray with a touch of blue. In many western locations Paradun and No Hackle imitations colored to match the Blue Winged Olive hatch are the only patterns you need to carry for early season fishing. If you are familiar with the size of the mayflies that hatch in your area the number of imitations that you need to carry for size matching is cut down significantly.

Third: The kind of water that you most often fish is an important factor in reducing the number of patterns needed to match the hatch. If you fish only fast-moving streams with a lot of broken water, you eliminate the need to carry Paradun or No Hackle imitations. You will only need to carry impressionistic mayfly patterns like the Adams, Light Cahill, Quill Gordon, House & Lot and Gray Wulff.

These three suggestions should help you cut down the number of patterns that you need to match the hatch to a manageable number. It's no fun if you need a pack mule to carry around your fly box.

FISHING MAYFLY IMITATIONS ON SPRING CREEKS

Spring creeks, like the mythical Greek God Zenus, are born full grown, pushed to life by underground springs. Unlike other trout streams, spring creeks are not directly dependent upon rainfall and snow run off for their life blood. Spring creeks receive most of their water from large underground reservoirs that have accumulated their water from the precipitation of many seasons. Spring creeks, unless they have many rain and snow fed tributaries, are not subject to the extremes of flow fluctuation as are rain and snow fed rivers. Montana's famous spring creek, Armstrong Spring Creek, remains at about the same flow year round. On the other hand, the Big Hole River in Montana, during the June snow melt, can turn into a raging torrent and by September usually flows at about one-tenth of the June flow.

Due to their underground origin, spring creeks are less subject to discoloration than are rain and snow fed streams. During June when many streams and rivers in the West are unfishable because of discoloration and high water, spring creeks without major tributaries run clear.

Some spring creeks have very slow moving currents while others move very fast. However, a spring creek will usually have a smooth, clear and unbroken flow. The clear, unbroken water of most spring creeks give trout the clarity of observation that enables them to closely examine an imitation. In those spring creeks that have a slow current, the trout is given an added advantage — time. Time to drift leisurely along under your fly to detect anything the least bit unnatural. Spring creek fishing usually means "match the hatch" fishing. The first step in attempting to match the hatch is to collect a sample of the insect on which the trout are feeding.

Most fishermen rig up, rush to the stream and start flailing the water with their fly. This is a serious mistake. Always collect a sample before starting to fish. In order to collect a sample you will need a small net. A small aquarium net or small homemade net of fine mesh wire will work great. Make sure that the mayfly that you have collected is the insect on which the trout are feeding. This becomes very important in those situations where there is a multiple hatch. It does no good to go to the trouble of collecting a sample if the insect that you collect is not of the type on which the trout are feeding.

Another method of collecting a sample is to use a stomach pump. This method, of course, requires you to catch a trout. This may take some time if you are using the wrong size and color fly to begin with. However, in using the stomach pump you have one important advantage over the net method. You know that you have a sample of what the trout are actually eating. If you use a stomach pump, use it gently as follows: first inject a small amount of water into the fish prior to suction. Next, deflate the bulb, slide the tube gently into the throat of the trout just slightly further down than the gills (never put the tube into the stomach of a trout as this will produce serious damage). Now let the bulb inflate; the air rushing in to fill the vacuum in the bulb will carry with it the insects on which the trout has been recently feeding.

Once you have captured a sample, examine it closely. Many fly shops sell a small plastic box with a low powered magnifying glass built into the top lid which is very helpful for this purpose. Next, check the body and wing coloration of your sample and measure the size of the mayfly with a milla-gauge. If you don't have a milla-gauge (most people don't) size the natural to a fly in your box. Size is very important. If the naturals on which the trout are feeding are size 20 and the fly that you are using is a size 14, there is a whopping size variation of 60%. Size variations and drag account for more refusals than any other factors. Make sure that your artificial and the natural are the same size.

Matching the correct silhouette of the natural is also very important. The reason I recommend Paraduns or No Hackle flies or the Parks-Wilson fly (discussed later) for the finicky trout on most spring creek fishing situations is because the hackle on conventional flies tends to obscure the silhouette of the wing. Wings are the part of the mayfly that the trout sees first. If the trout's view of the wings is obstructed by hackle, it will more than likely respond negatively.

A close examination of a natural mayfly reveals that the natural sits much lower in the water than the traditional hackle fly that is designed to float with only the hackle points and tail touching the water. Removal of the hackle or tying the hackle parallel to the water as with the Paradun and Parachute style flies, gives a fly a much more natural float and presents a better wing silhouette to the trout.

No Hackle flies have been tied for years. However, they were recently popularized by Doug Swisher and Carl Richards in their excellent book *Selective Trout.* While standard No Hackle flies work well for the selective trout found on most spring creeks, I have found that by adding legs to the standard pattern the number of strikes increases significantly. Mayfly imitations tied parachute or paradun style with the hackle tied parallel to the water are designed to represent legs. However, the numerous hackle points touching the water creates the impression that the fly has many more legs than the natural.

The Parks-Wilson, tied with six individual legs, gives a more realistic mayfly silhouette than the standard No Hackle, Paradun or Parachute style mayfly imitation. This pattern's single wing construction presents a better mayfly wing silhouette than the standard dual winged No Hackle. Examination of natural mayflies in the dun stage reveals that they float with their wings together or so close together as to be imperceptible to the trout. The great tier, Theodore Gordon, was one of the first to recognize this by tying the original Quill Gordon with one upright wing.

During our field tests performed on slow moving spring creeks, the Parks-Wilson out performed both the Paradun and No Hackle style flies. Our field tests were conducted under the following conditions: First, trout rising to mayflies were located. Next, a sample of the mayfly on which the trout were feeding was collected. The test flies (Paradun, No Hackle and the Parks-Wilson) were then colored with Pantone marking pens to represent the colors of the natural. The legs of the Parks-Wilson were also colored to match the leg color of the natural. Next we drifted each of the flies over the rising fish, keeping track of the number of strikes. Casts that were not properly performed (those that were outside the feeding lanes, where the No Hackle fly floated on its side or where drag developed) were not entered in our tally. The results showed in test after test that the Parks-Wilson received approximately 20% more strikes than the Paradun and 40% more strikes than the No Hackle fly. We realize that it is impossible to perform a perfectly controlled test and that some readers may be skeptical of the results. To those readers we say "conduct your own test."

Hackle flies have their place on rough, fast-moving water where their advantage of floating high and being easier to see outweighs poor wing and body silhouette and unnatural floating angle.

The next step is to impart to your imitation the behavior of the natural. Presentation on spring creeks is critical. I generally prefer the downstream cast when fishing these streams. To accomplish a downstream cast, first cast downstream and slightly across. Feed line out by pointing the rod tip toward the water at about a 45 degree angle, then shake the rod tip so that the line feeds out fast enough to allow the fly to keep up with the current and float drag free. In order to get long, drag free floats, you must occasionally mend the line. Mending is accomplished by flipping the belly of the line upstream without any interruption to the natural float of your fly.

The downstream cast method gives you certain advantages over the traditional upstream cast. First, the trout does not see your line or leader before the fly is presented. This is important with the leader-conscious trout found on many spring creeks. More importantly, you can achieve much longer drag-free floats by using this method. Floats of 15 to 30 feet are not uncommon. However, there are certain problems with the downstream cast which you should keep in mind. Unless you are a careful wader, you may kick up debris from the bottom of the stream which will float downstream and signal your presence to the trout. To avoid this problem, whenever possible, fish spring creeks from the bank or a boat. Remember to walk lightly along the bank as ground vibration transmitted into the water by tree roots, grass roots and the ground itself will often put rising fish down.

When fishing downstream, there is a greater danger of being seen by the trout. Trout always face upstream with their head pointed into the current. Most authorities agree that trout can see between 10 and 30 feet upstream depending on their depth in the water. Remember the old adage — if you can see them, they can see you. The lower you stay to the water the less likely you are to be seen. It is helpful to wear dark clothing as it does not reflect as much light. Prevent your shadow and especially moving shadows like your rod from crossing a rising fish. Moving shadows signal a predatory attack like that of an Osprey. A shadow falling across a feeding fish will normally cause it to scurry downstream putting other fish down.

Hooking fish is more difficult when fishing downstream due to the fact that when you set the hook you are pulling the fly away from the upstream-facing fish. You must learn to hold off striking until the fish starts to angle down below the surface.

When casting to a rising fish, especially on a spring creek, it is important to cast above the rise. Trout normally lie above where the rise takes place. Trout drift along under a fly examining it before the strike is made. A cast made to the point of the rise will usually not be seen by the trout as the fly will fall behind the fish and out of its line of vision. On smooth water a good rule of thumb is to cast at least 10 feet above the rise point.

Often there is a definite and consistent period of time between the rises of a particular fish. It is not unusual to observe a feeding trout that will rise at precise intervals. When this occurs, flies that float through a trout's feeding lane that do not coincide with the rhythm or interval of the rise will not be taken. The trick is to present your fly so that it reaches the trout's feeding station at the time the trout is again ready to feed. Should your timing be off, let the fly float well past where the trout has been feeding before gently taking the line off the water. A mistake that many fishermen make is that they take the line off the water too abruptly and too close to the trout's feeding station, thereby putting the fish down. Keep casting until the trout's feeding rhythm and your fly coincide.

Leader diameter is especially important when dealing with leader-conscious spring creek trout. Six and 7X tippets are advisable for most spring creek fishing. I prefer leaders of at least 12 feet. On some streams you can get away with 5X and sometimes even 4X tippets, but I have found that the number of strikes decreases significantly when using the heavier tippet material. Some fishermen even prefer to use 8X for very leader-conscious trout. According to one sage fisherman, the only chance one has to land a good fish hooked on 8X is to starve it to death. Every time the hooked trout goes after a fly, the story goes, you pull very gently on your line causing the hooked fish to slightly miss the surface morsel. This goes on for days until the fish finally starves to exhaustion and it is landed.

When using 6, 7 and 8X tippet material you will experience fewer broken tippets if you use tippets of at least three feet in length. Long tippets make it more difficult to turn over the fly but the long length takes up the shock on the initial strike when the danger of getting broken off is greatest. Short tippets under 18 inches, when fishing with 6, 7 or 8X, almost invariably break on the strike or the initial run. For most spring creek fishing I prefer to use 4 and 5 weight lines and a long rod, preferably at least 9 feet.

FISHING MAYFLY IMITATIONS ON RAIN AND SNOW FED STREAMS AND RIVERS

Rain and snow fed streams, unlike most spring creeks, are subject to great variation in flow and to discoloration.

Many of these kinds of streams are unfishable in the early season because of high, murky water. Rivers like the Yellowstone, Snake, Big Hole, Madison and Colorado are seldom fishable because of high water until at least the last week of June.

Snow and rain fed streams, especially early in the season, are normally characterized by swift, broken water. On this kind of water visibility and high float are more important than faithful imitation. For this reason, I seldom use No Hackle patterns or Paraduns but prefer mayfly hackled patterns that float well and sit high. This is not the same "match-the-hatch" fishing that you are likely to find on spring creeks. Trout in fast, broken water have little time to examine your fly and broken water obscures the trout's vision of your offering. However, it is still important to get a sample of what the trout are feeding on. Make sure that your artificial and the natural are matched correctly. Matching the coloration is not as important as it is on most spring creeks because fish in fast water get a limited examination time. The more impressionistic mayfly patterns work well on this kind of water.

The H&L Variant, also known as the House & Lot or the Eisenhower is one of my favorite mayfly imitations for fast water. Due to its tail and wing construction out of white calf's tail, it has excellent floatation characteristics and it is very easy to see. The fly has a general resemblance to many different species of mayflies. It works well no matter what kind of mayfly is on the water. This fly can be tied anywhere from size 10 to 20. Even in the small sizes it is an excellent floater and easy to see.

The Adams is one of the best all around dry fly imitations. Some argue that it represents a caddisfly. It works well for both insects. Because it has a resemblance to many different kinds of insects, it is a good pattern to use if you are not exactly sure what kind of insect hatch is taking place. One drawback of the Adams is that it is very difficult to see when fished on many of the swift turbulent rivers of the west. Its colors have a tendency to blend into the water. Instead of using the Adams tied in the traditional manner, I prefer to use the Adams tied irresistible style. This design, made of spun deer hair, gives the fly a higher float and greater visibility than the standard Adams.

The Light Cahill, Light Hendrickson and Quill Gordon are impressionistic mayfly patterns that also work well. If the mayfly is light in color, using a Light Cahill or Light Hendrickson of the appropriate size works fine. The Quill Gordon works well for the darker colored mayflies that make up many of the early season hatches.

The Gray Wulff is also an effective imitation for most of the dark colored mayflies. It works particularly well as an early season *Baetis* imitation.

The Mosquito is also an effective pattern because of its general resemblance to a mayfly. Trout rarely, if ever, feed on adult mosquitoes. The Mosquito works well, like the Gray Wulff, as a **Baetis** imitation. Some anglers also use the Mosquito as a fluttering caddis imitation.

The Charcoal Quill is another dark mayfly imitation. Its primary use is to match the tiny dark mayflies that hatch on many Rocky Mountain streams and rivers in the winter.

PRESENTATION

The traditional upstream presentation works best when fishing a mayfly imitation on fast, broken water. The conflicting currents attendant to swift water make drag difficult to prevent on most early season rain and snow fed streams. You must learn to throw a good slack line or "S" cast. Upstream casts should be kept short. Pull in slack line as the fly line floats toward you. At the same time hold the rod high so that you are in a position to make a back cast. As soon as the fly starts to drag, cast to the next fishing situation. Through a day's fishing, more productive water is covered using this technique than if you have to retrieve slack line after each cast. The downstream cast on this kind of water is very difficult to execute properly as it is almost impossible to feed out line fast enough to keep pace with a fast-moving current.

Fish in fast-flowing water are normally not as leader-conscious as trout in slower flowing water. Three and 4X tippet leaders usually work best. Leaders with a greater diameter tend to reduce the free movement of the fly. My line choice for dry fly fishing on rain and snow fed streams is a 6 or 7 weight line. My favorite rod length is at least 9 feet for this type of stream.

Some western mayfly hatches are so dependable and widespread that it is worth listing them. Hatch dates given are from our own observation and vary slightly depending on elevation, water conditions and temperature. We have not attempted to list all western mayfly hatches, only those which we feel are the most important.

Blue Winged Olive *(Baetis)*

This genus of mayfly is found all over the West from Colorado to California. Most species of this group have light gray to pale blue wings and a dark olive to gray body. This mayfly is small, ranging from hook sizes 18 to 24. It is important to remember that this fly usually makes up the first hatch of the season. In many western locations, the *Baetis* hatch will have started by the middle of April. I have even observed a *Baetis* hatch as early as February on the Merced River in California. The Adams, the Gray Wulff and Mosquito tied in small sizes and the No Hackle, Paradun and Parks-Wilson patterns tied in the appropriate colors serve as good imitations. *Baetis* mayflies usually float on the surface for a long distance before the early spring sun warms them enough to allow them to take flight. This species of mayfly is especially vulnerable to trout. Even if the water temperature of the stream is very cold, trout will usually be brought to the surface by an early season *Baetis* hatch. This hatch normally takes place in the afternoon during the warmest time of the day. *Baetis* mayflies are found on both slow and fast moving streams.

Freckled Dun *(Callabaetis)*

This genus of mayfly is usually found on lakes or slow moving streams. The body of the dun has a freckled appearance and the wings have dark splotches making this species of mayfly easy to identify. This mayfly is best matched by hook sizes 14 to 18.

Most of the important species of this genus hatch between May and the last of June. There hasn't as yet been a specific western pattern developed to match the *Callabaetis*. It is best to collect a sample and then color a white bodied, light winged No Hackle, Paradun or Parks-Wilson pattern to match the appearance of the natural.

The most common body color is olive with a tinge of brown. Wing color is usually dark gray.

Western Green Drake *(Ephemerella grandis)*

The Green Drake hatch is one of the most important hatches in the West. This mayfly has a greenish-olive body and light gray wings. The Green Drake is huge. Ideal hook size is No. 6.

This hatch on many western rivers rivals the salmonfly hatch in importance. During this hatch, large trout that seldom feed on the surface, are brought to the top to feast on the juicy greenish-lime bug. If you fish this hatch on one of the more popular western rivers, chances are you will not be alone. Anglers on Henry's Fork of the Snake line up almost shoulder to shoulder during this hatch.

This hatch usually starts on Henry's Fork around June 25. On the Pacific Slope streams, the hatch is normally under way by the middle of June. The hatch lasts for approximately two weeks.

An Adams Irresistible tied with deer hair dyed light green and with light green dyed grizzly hackle is a very effective imitation for the Green Drake.

Olive Duns *(Ephemerella flavilinea)*

This mayfly has an olive green body and dark gray wings. It looks much like a small green drake.

This insect is best matched by hook sizes 12 to 16. The hatch usually begins around June 25 and lasts until the middle of August. In most localities this hatch immediately follows the green drake hatch.

Pale Morning Duns (Genus *Ephemerella infrequens and inermis*)

These two species of mayflies are found in great abundance on almost every western trout stream. The species *E. infrequen* has a pale yellow or almost cream body with light pale lemon wings. This species is best matched by hook sizes 16 to 20. The body of the *E. inermis* is olive with a tinge of yellow and the wings are darker than the *E. infrequen*. The *E. inermis* is smaller than the *E. infrequen* and is best matched by hook sizes 20 to 22. Hatch time for both species is usually around midday. The period of the emergence is of long duration. The hatch usually starts in early June and lasts until the start of October.

Tricorythodes

This specie of mayfly hatches on the slow, alkaline rich water found on many western spring creeks. I have not observed this mayfly on any fast moving streams. This insect is very small and best matched by hook sizes 24-28. Its body color is dark brown to almost black. Its wings are white and its legs are light in color. This mayfly species has only one pair of wings, lacking the small hind pair found on most mayfly species. Emergence in most western locations takes place during August and September.

Tricorythodes mayflies make a rapid transformation, normally in a few minutes, from the dun stage to the spinner stage. During this insect's hatching period both spinners and duns will be present. At the start of the hatch the trout will normally be keyed to the tiny duns. The duns are best imitated by a No Hackle or Paradun pattern tied with a dark body and white wings. It is important to add another tail to the standard pattern as this insect has three white tails. Tail length should be long — at least one and one-half the length of the body.

Once the hatch is well under way, trout begin switching their preference to the arriving spinners. The *Tricorythodes* Poly Winged Spinner is an effective imitation.

IMPORTANT POINTS TO REMEMBER

1. Mayflies have upright wings and look like tiny sailboats when drifting in the current.
2. The wings of a spinner are almost transparent. Tail length is about twice the length of that of the dun stage.
3. Memorize the 13 mayfly rules.
4. Always collect a sample before starting to fish.
5. More refusals take place because of size variation than any other factor in hatch matching.
6. On most spring creeks the downstream cast works best. On most rain and snow fed streams the traditional upstream cast works best.
7. Walk lightly along the bank of a stream or river as ground vibration transmitted into the water by tree roots, grass roots and the ground itself will often put rising fish down.
8. Prevent your shadow or the moving shadow of your rod from crossing a rising fish.
9. When casting to a rising fish on smooth water cast at least 10 feet above the rise point.
10. When fishing with 6, 7 or 8X tippet material use tippets of at least three feet in length. Long tippets take up the shock on the initial strike and run.
11. The more you learn about streamside entomology the better fly fisherman you will become. Become familiar with the major mayfly hatches that take place in the West.

ADAMS

ACCORDING to Smedley in *Fly Patterns and Their Origins,* the Adams was first tied about 1922 by Leonard Halladay of Michigan who gave it to Mr. C. F. Adams to try in a nearby stream. Its success was immediate. Adams felt that the fly bearing his name was at its best as a representation of the flying ant, though he caught fish under any conditions.

I have my doubts about the ant theory but there is no question that the Adams represents a multiple threat. It has the basic silhouette of the mayfly and the color tones of the caddis. This multiplicity of options is doubtless one of the reasons for the fly's continual success, especially in those situations characterized by mixed hatches of mayflies and caddisflies.

HOOK:	94840, sizes 12-14; 94838, sizes 16-18.
THREAD:	Black 3/0 mono-cord.
TAIL:	Brown and grizzly hackle fibers.
BODY:	Dubbed muskrat or substitute.
WING:	Grizzly hackle points.
HACKLE:	Brown and grizzly neck hackle.

1. Strip several grizzly hackle fibers from a large feather, and an equal group from a brown hackle for the tail. Be careful to get the tips aligned so that the tail has a uniform end. Attach the hackle-fiber tail to the hook.

2. Select two matching grizzly hackle points for the wings. Pair the two feather points together with the shiny sides together and the dull sides out, so that the feathers curve away from each other. Attach the wings to the hook.

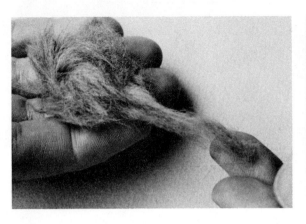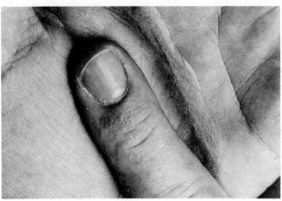

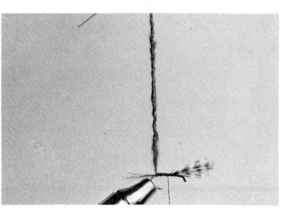

3. Pull a small strand of fur out of the fur ball for the body. Make a loop of the thread by pulling it off the bobbin and winding the thread back over the loop toward the tail. This loop of thread becomes the dubbing loop. Varnish or wax the dubbing loop and place the prepared fur strand between the threads of the loop. Spin the dubbing thread so as to make a yarn out of the thread and fur.

4. Use the hackle pliers to wind the body just as if it were any other yarn body.

5. Pull the wings back and erect them by placing several turns of the thread against their base. Divide the wings by placing figure 8's between them.

6. Select a brown hackle and a grizzly hackle for the fly. Wind each hackle individually. Shape the head, whip finish, and cement.

GRAY WULFF

THE Gray Wulff and the White Wulff were the first two patterns in this extensive series. Lee Wulff tied this fly to represent the large gray drake of New York's rough Ausable River in 1929. By intention it is a mayfly type well suited to heavy water.

Mr. Wulff advises against the tendency to reduce the size of the fly. The flat water situations which require a small fly are better fished with a more exact imitation. On rough water however, fish tend to be much less selective allowing a more impressionistic fly such as the Wulff to succeed.

HOOK:	94840, sizes 8-14.
THREAD:	Black 3/0 mono-cord.
TAIL:	Brown bucktail.
BODY:	Gray poly yarn.
WING:	Brown bucktail.
HACKLE:	Blue dun saddle hackle and neck hackle.

1. Cut hair from the base of a brown bucktail for the tail. Attach the tail to the hook with four turns of thread.

2. Cut more hair, about twice as much as used in the tail, from the bucktail for the wings. Attach the wing to the hook with four turns of the thread.

3. Polypropylene yarn, like spun fur, can be divided into three separate strands. Secure one of these strands to the hook. Wind the body segment, being careful to get this good and tight. The poly material is slightly elastic, so go ahead and stretch it while forming the body.

4. Erect the wings by pulling the wing back and laying six turns of thread against the base. Divide your wings and lay two figure 8's between the two wing segments. Make a three-turn collar around the base of each wing. End with the thread behind the wings. Place a small drop of cement between the wings to seal that area.

5. Select one blue dun saddle hackle and one blue dun neck hackle of the size appropriate for the hook. Wind the hackles one at a time, making turns both behind and ahead of the wings. Tie the hackles off with two turns of thread. Whip finish and cement the head.

LIGHT CAHILL

THE Light Cahill ranks with the Quill Gordon as one of America's first and finest contributions to the history of the dry fly. The fly was originated by Mr. Cahill of New York, prior to 1882. This fly has been produced with numerous variations and new materials.

I use fitch for the dubbing on these light cream bodied flies. However, several other furs can be substituted. The light belly underfur of the fox is probably the most common. Cream spun fur or poly yarn is frequently used. Poly dubbing material can also be used.

On this fly, as on other conventional mayfly patterns, I shift to the 94838 hook for sizes 16 and smaller. The standard 94840 looks more like a long shank in the smaller sizes.

This fly is in the classic mayfly tradition and can be used with success on most waters undergoing an appropriate hatch.

HOOK:	94840, sizes 12-14; 94838, sizes 16-18.
THREAD:	Yellow 3/0 mono-cord.
TAIL:	Light ginger hackle fibers.
BODY:	Dubbed fitch.
WING:	Woodduck or mallard dyed to substitute.
HACKLE:	Light ginger neck hackle.

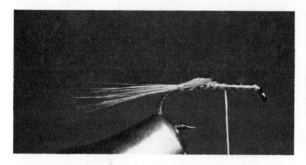

1. Strip the ginger hackle fibers required for the tail from the stem of the feather. Attach the tail to the hook with one or two turns of thread.

2. The wing on the Light Cahill is a wood-duck flank feather or a mallard dyed to simulate woodduck. Attach the wing with four turns of the thread.

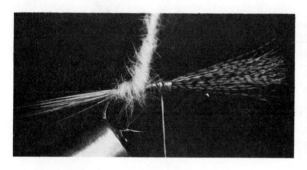

3. Using the loop technique, dub the fitch body material.

4. Using the hackle pliers, wind the body onto the hook.

5. Erect and divide the wings. Wrap a three-turn collar around each wing base.

6. Prepare two light ginger neck hackles. Face the dull sides together and secure them to the hook. Wind the hackle feathers one at a time. Shape the head, whip finish, and lacquer.

LIGHT HENDRICKSON

THE Hendrickson was first tied in 1916 by Roy Steenrod, confidant of the great Theodore Gordon. According to Smedley's account in *Fly Patterns and Their Origins,* Steenrod tied the original to represent a particular mayfly, perhaps *E. Subvaria*, hatching on New York's Beaverkill River. The *E. Subvaria* does not occur in the West, but other mayflies exhibiting these general color tones do. The most common of these are the *E. Infrequens* which can also be represented by the Pale Evening Dun pattern (even though the *Infrequens* is a morning dun).

The original dressing was the Dark Hendrickson and was tied with a tail of golden pheasant tippet. Today we use blue dun hackle fibers, though some prefer hair tails. Spun fur, poly yarns, or any cream dubbing fur or poly material may be used to make the body.

HOOK:	94840, sizes 12 and 14; 94838, sizes 16-18.
THREAD:	Yellow mono-cord.
TAIL:	Light blue dun hackle fibers.
BODY:	Dubbed cream fur.
WING:	Woodduck or mallard flank feathers dyed to substitute.
HACKLE:	Light blue dun neck hackle.

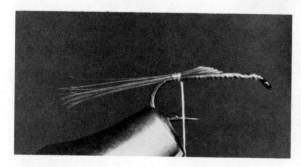

1. Select a light blue dun hackle for the tail. Strip a group of barbules off the hackle stem and secure with three turns of thread.

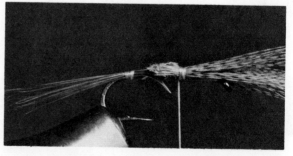

2. The wing material is mallard dyed to simulate woodduck. Strip the barbules from the stem of the feather to form the wing. Position the wing on the hook and secure it with four turns of thread.

84

3. Make a fur strand for the body. Varnish or wax the dubbing thread. Place the fur strand between the threads of the dubbing loop and spin it until the yarn is well formed. Hold the prepared yarn with the hackle pliers and wind the body.

4. Erect the wing by pulling it back and laying several turns of thread in front of the wing. Divide the wing with figure 8's. Place a small drop of varnish or cement between the wing. Select two light blue dun hackles for the hackle. Face the hackles with the shiny sides out and the dull sides togehter. Wind the hackles one at a time, securing each hackle with one or two turns of the tying thread. Whip finish and cement.

HAIRWING VARIANT

THE Hairwing Variant was derived from the House & Lot about 1960 by my late father, Merton Parks. The House & Lot was a Colorado pattern originally popularized as President Eisenhower's favorite fly.

The principal point of difference between our flies and the usual dressings is that the Hairwing Variant is commonly dressed quite heavily as if it were a Wulff, while ours is ultra-sparse. The standard dressing is an effective rough water fly, certainly one of the best rough water mayfly imitations. By dressing the fly sparsely it becomes a very effective fly on flat water. Time and again we have found it to be a better producer than specific imitations when fishing multi-species hatches. Another endearing feature is its ability to look like a No. 16 to the fish below but a No. 12 to the fisherman trying to find it in poor light conditions.

HOOK:	94840, Sizes 12-18.
THREAD:	Black 3/0 mono-cord.
TAIL:	White calf tail — sparse and variant.
BODY:	Stripped peacock quill.
RIB:	Light olive or tan thread, or gold wire.
WING:	White calf tail — sparse, erect and divided.
HACKLE:	Furnace saddle — sparse.

1. Clip a small group of fibers from the calf tail for the tail of the fly and secure. Keep the tail sparse, since the essence of this fly is lightness.

2. Clip more calf tail for the wing and prepare it in the usual way. Sparse is still the watchword. The wing material should equal twice the tail in quantity. Attach the wing to the hook.

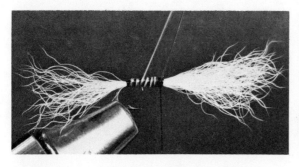

3. Tie in the ribbing thread and stripped quill section with one or two turns of thread for each. Wind the quill, followed by the ribbing thread.

4. Erect the wing and separate with figure 8's. Wrap a three-turn collar around each wing base.

5. Select a furnace saddle hackle and attach it to the hook. Wind the hackle, using only about six turns of the hackle feather — two behind the wing and four in front of it.

6. Shape and whip finish the head of the fly. Lacquer both the head and the body.

NO-COLOR PARACHUTE

T WO conflicting theories justify the development of parachute patterns. The first is that the horizontally wound hackle is heavily dressed to act as a parachute. (William Brush of Detroit took out a patent on the method which was granted in September of 1934.) The second theory views the parachute as a realistic solution to the problem of how to represent the legs on mayflies. As described in *Selective Trout* and elsewhere, the essence of this approach is to keep the hackle sparse. In our view this approach is more useful than the original.

HOOK:	94838, sizes 14-18.
THREAD:	Cream 6/0 pre-waxed.
TAIL:	Two light elk body hairs.
BODY:	Cream poly yarn or dubbing.
WING:	Light elk body hair in a single post.
HACKLE:	Sparse cream neck hackle.

1. Separate a length of spun fur into its three component strands. Attach one of these strands to the hook with four turns of the thread. Either natural or poly dubbing can be used.

2. Cut two light elk body hairs from the hide and attach them on either side of the body so that they are split.

3. Cut more elk hair from the hide. Attach this hair for the wing.

4. Erect the wing and wrap three-turn collars at wing bases.

5. Wind the remainder of the body up to and past the wing to the head position.

6. Select a cream hackle feather and attach it to the hook at the base of the wing. The shiny side of the feather must face you so that the natural curve of the barbules will face down when the hackle is wound. Wind five turns of the hackle feather in a counter-clockwise direction around the base of the wing. (The hackle must be wound counter-clockwise or it will prove difficult to secure.) Whip finish and cement.

QUILL GORDON

SMEDLEY's excellent little book, *Fly Patterns and Their Origins*, now out of print, gives us the most likely original dressing for this fly. Theodore Gordon did not divide his wings, suggesting that a single wing gave a more accurate silhouette. He observed that natural mayflies carry their wings erect and together as duns, and flat out as spinners. His original dressing apparently used woodduck for the tail as well as the wing. He reinforced the quill body with gold wire. By 1960 DuBois was able to list in *The Fisherman's Handbook of Trout Flies* thirty-two variations on Gordon's original theme.

A large percentage of mayflies on most western waters, other than spring creeks, are dark mayflies. The Quill Gordon is not an exact imitation of any of them, but in appropriate sizes resembles most of them. Mixed hatches are quite common and a generalized pattern like this gives the fish room to make unwise conclusions.

HOOK:	94840, sizes 12 and 14; 94838, sizes 16 and 18.
THREAD:	Black mono-cord.
TAIL:	Blue dun hackle fibers.
BODY:	Stripped peacock quill.
RIB:	Light olive or tan thread or gold wire.
WING:	Woodduck flank or mallard dyed woodduck.
HACKLE:	Blue dun neck.

1. Strip some blue dun hackle fibers from the stem of a large hackle. Attach the tail at the bend of the hook.

2. Bear in mind that these flies are getting fairly small and you don't want too much wing material. Attach the wing to the fly with the wing material out over the eye of the fly.

3. Tie in the ribbing and a single stripped peacock quill.

4. Coat the body with Duco and wind the quill into the fresh cement. Be sure to leave just a little strip of black showing between each turn of the quill. Tie the quill off, then wind the rib right on top of the quill.

5. Erect and divide the wings by the usual process.

6. A small drop of lacquer should be applied between the wings to seal that unit and a second liberal coat of Duco applied over the body. Select two blue dun neck hackles of the appropriate size. Secure them to the hook behind the wings.

7. Wind the hackles one at a time. Tie these hackles off with a couple turns of the tying thread. Shape the head, whip finish, and cement.

CHARCOAL QUILL

THIS fly was first tied in the winter of 1955 by my father, Merton Parks. Tied to represent the very dark winter mayflies of the Yellowstone, probably *Baetis*, it also serves as a snow-fly imitation. These snowflies are little *Diptera*, so named because they appear on the streamside snow and ice pans. Winter afternoons are frequently marked by both hatches and freely rising fish.

The fly is in all respects like the Quill Gordon except for the use of the color charcoal for the tail and hackle. This color is obtained by dyeing ordinary brown necks green. Care must be taken not to over-dye, as a really black-black can result. The idea is to achieve a color almost, but not quite, black.

HOOK:	93838, sizes 16-18.
THREAD:	Black 7/0 pre-waxed.
TAIL:	Charcoal hackle fibers.
BODY:	Stripped peacock quill.
RIB:	Tan or light olive thread, or gold wire.
WING:	Woodduck or mallard dyed to simulate woodduck.
HACKLE:	Charcoal neck hackle.

1. The tail for this fly is charcoal colored neck hackle. The hackle fibers are stripped from the stem of the feather. Secure these fibers to the hook with two turns of the thread.

2. The wing is mallard dyed to simulate woodduck. Strip the fibers for the wing from the stem of the feather. Take care to avoid excessive wing bulk. Secure the wing to the hook with three turns of thread.

3. Cement the butts of the wings and tail. Tie in a single strand of tan 3/0 mono-cord as a rib for the quill body, and a single strand of stripped peacock quill. Place a layer of cement on the body and wind the quill through it. Then wind the ribbing thread on the quill and secure it.

4. Pull the wing back and erect it with several turns of thread against its base. Divide the wings and tie figure 8's between them. Wrap a three-turn collar around each wing base.

5. Select two charcoal neck hackles. Wind each hackle with some behind the wing and some in front. Shape the head, whip finish, and lacquer.

MOSQUITO

THE continuing popularity of the Mosquito is based on a general resemblance to fluttering caddis and mayflies. Evidence indicates that fish seldom, if ever, eat adult mosquitoes. The fly is especially popular in California where, as elsewhere, many streams have *Baetis* mayfly hatches that can be represented by the Mosquito's gray tones.

The most widely used alternative pattern is the California Mosquito which has a red tail. Our dressing uses white moose mane over black thread to create the body but other combinations are possible. Some of these alternatives are a black thread rib on white floss, a regular stripped peacock quill, black and white thread, and stripped hackle stem quill bodies.

HOOK:	94840, sizes 12-14; 94838, sizes 16-18.
THREAD:	Black 3/0 mono-cord.
TAIL:	Grizzly hackle fibers.
BODY:	White moose mane.
WING:	Grizzly hackle tips.
HACKLE:	Grizzly neck hackle.

1. The tail is grizzly hackle fiber stripped from a large feather. Attach these with three turns of the thread.

2. Select two grizzly hackles of about the same shape and color pattern to make the hackle point wings. Face the feathers so that the curves face away from each other. Secure the wings to the hook with three turns of thread.

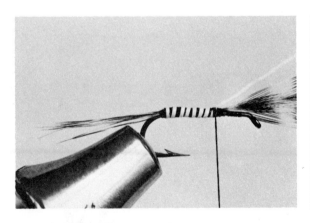

3. Select a single strand of white moose mane. Liberally cement the body. Wind the moose mane carefully, leaving an equal space of black thread showing between the turns of the white moose mane strand.

4. Erect and divide the wings. Place a drop of lacquer between the wings, and a second layer of cement on the body. Select two grizzly hackles. Wind the hackles one at a time, starting with at least one turn behind the wings and then coming around in front of the wings. Shape the head, whip finish, and cement.

POLY-WING SPINNER

THE fragility of many spinner patterns combined with their complexity discourages much experimentation with imitations of this phase of the mayfly life cycle. Yet spinners remain a significant part of the trout's diet, especially on those streams with a massive *Tricorythodes* hatch.

The advent of the polypropolene materials made possible the development of a series of spinner imitations that were simple in concept and physically strong. The dressing given below for the *Tricorythodes* spinner can easily be modified to represent almost any spinner by changing the body, tail and wing color tones appropriately.

HOOK:	94838, sizes 16-20.
THREAD:	Black 6/0 mono-cord.
TAIL:	Two light elk hairs.
BODY:	Black spun fur — single strand.
WING:	Poly yarn strand tied spinner style.
HACKLE:	None.

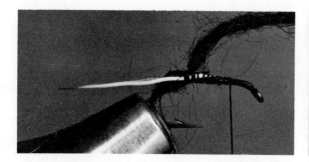

1. Separate a piece of spun fur into its three strands and attach one of them to the hook. Make a single turn of the yarn at the tail and tie it off on top of the hook. Attach a single light elk body hair on each side of the body getting a good spread. Tails should be the same length as the hook.

2. Separate a strand of white poly yarn into three parts. Attach the center of the poly wing to the hook at the wing position. Secure it with a pair of figure 8 turns of thread, leaving the wings flat out in the spinner position.

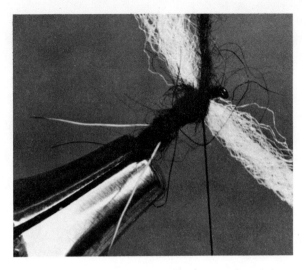

3. Wind the body starting with a turn right up against the tails. Make a figure 8 between the wings to build up the thorax. Shape the head, whip finish, and cement.

THE BASTARD (MIDGE)

THIS fly was first tied by my father, Merton Parks, about 1955 for Jack Rose of Gardiner, Montana, a local fisherman of considerable skill. He wanted a fly to represent the little dark *Diptera*, commonly called snowflies throughout the West. He reported excellent results but allowed that "seeing the little bastard was tough." This was no wonder as this is a surface film fly rather than a true floater.

The way it floats and its general outline seemed suggestive of spinner mayflies and emergers, thus prompting me to apply the design to other flies. One uses blue dun hackle and gray spun fur to represent the gray tones and a second employs yellow thread, cream spun fur, light hair and light ginger hackle to match these natural tones. The resulting blue and ginger midges could easily be adapted to other color schemes.

HOOK: 94838, sizes 16-20.
THREAD: Black 6/0 pre-waxed.

BODY:	Black spun fur.
HACKLE:	Charcoal neck hackle — trimmed.
SHELLBACK:	Dark deer body hair.
TAIL:	Dark deer body hair.

1. Since a strand of thread is required at the tail to secure the hair for both back and tail, tie it in now. Attach one strand of black spun fur to the hook at the bend.

2. Wind the body yarn, tying it off with three turns of thread.

3. Secure a large charcoal neck feather for the hackle. Wind the hackle, tying it off with four turns of thread.

4. Gather the hackle below the hook. Let the hackle barbules that want to stand up do so. Then trim those fibers which extend above the hook.

5. Cut a dozen or so dark deer body hairs from the hide and attach. The tips should extend beyond the hook one shank length to form the tail. Whip finish the head.

6. Pull the back hair down to the bend of the hook. Whip finish the thread securing the tail. Trim the side barbules.

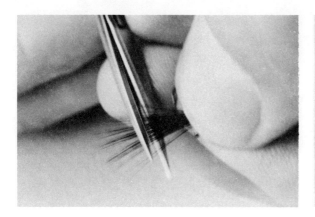

7. Trim off those barbules which extend below the hook. Complete the fly by cementing both the head and the thread at the tail.

NO-COLOR SIDEWINDER

THE Sidewinder is the best version of the standard patterns tied without hackle. Rene Harrop and Mike Lawson deserve major credit for the evolution of these flies. By using two sets of wing quills on each side of the fly, they have made a fly which is more durable than the regular pattern. This fly presents the four-wing silhouette of the natural mayfly.

By tying the fly without any commitment to color one has the option to color it later with Pantone pens.

HOOK:	94838, sizes 16-20.
THREAD:	Cream 6/0 pre-waxed.
TAIL:	Two light elk hairs.
BODY:	Cream poly yarn or dubbing.
WING:	White duck wing quills

1. Divide a section of spun fur yarn into three separate strands and secure one of these strands with four turns of thread. The same thing can be done with poly yarns. Make six turns of thread right at the bend of the hook to build up a hump of thread.

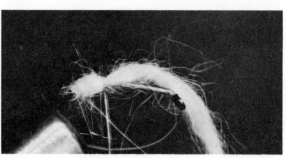

2. Make a single turn of the spun yarn onto the hump of thread.

3. Select two light elk hairs for the split tails. Attach them on either side of the body segment.

4. Wind the body yarn and tie it off with three turns of the thread.

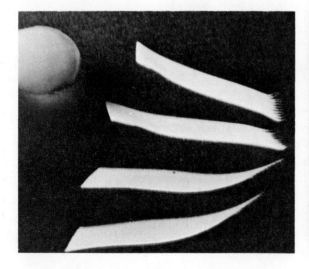

5. Trim two pairs of wings from the quills. These wings should be quite wide.

6. Match the two pairs of wings and tie them to the sides of the hook so that they are at an angle of 45 degrees.

7. Secure the wings with close turns of the thread.

8. Wind the remainder of the body. Shape the head, whip finish, and cement.

PARKS-WILSON

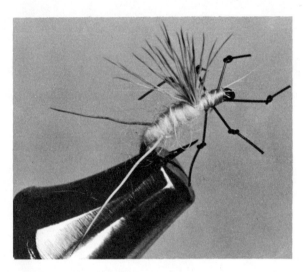

T HE inspiration for this fly is Bob Wilson's. The rationale is simple. If it is good to tempt selective fish with a fly tied without hackle to reveal the wing silhouette, then it ought to be even better to include legs. The result is a fly with a very naturalistic appearance. In our field tests it out-fished the standard No Hackle and Parachute.

As with other flies in this selection, it is tied here without any dominant color scheme. Different body colors or wing materials could easily be used to establish a color pattern. The Pantone pens can also be used to affect the colors. Hairs of other colors can be used for the legs as well. Patience, dexterity and a tolerance for frustration are recommended for tying this fly, especially in sizes smaller than 16.

HOOK:	94838, sizes 12-16.
THREAD:	Cream 6/0 pre-waxed.
TAIL:	Two light elk body hairs.
BODY:	Cream poly yarn or dubbing.
WING:	Light elk hair in a single post.
LEGS:	Three sets of knotted hairs or dyed monofilament.

1. Split a length of spun fur yarn into separate strands and attach one of these to the hook with four turns of thread. Make a single turn of the yarn, tying it off with two turns of thread.

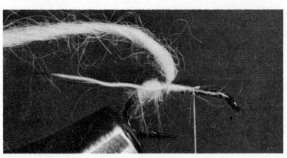

2. Select two light elk hairs for the tail and attach them on either side of the hook.

3. Clip a small group of light elk hairs from the hide. Attach the wing to the hook, trimming the butt at a slant.

4. Place Duco into the butt of the wing and secure it. Erect the wing and wrap a three-turn collar around each wing base.

5. Complete the body by winding the yarn forward past the wing to the head position. Secure the yarn, trim the excess, and then remove the hook from the vise. Replace the hook upside down in the vise.

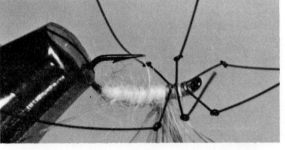

6. Cut three sections of dyed monofilament about two inches long, or select three long dark hairs from a moose mane. In each one tie a pair of overhand knots. The two knots need to be approximately 3/16 of an inch apart for a size 16 fly. Secure the first set of legs right under the wing segment, tying them in a "V" so that the legs both point backwards. The second leg goes right straight across, with a figure 8 of the tying thread securing it to the hook. The third leg goes on in a forward "V" position. Return the hook to the normal position. Trim the legs, whip finish, and cement.

Chapter VII

Directory of Dry Flies
and
Fly Shops in the West

ADAMS (Calf Tail Wing)
Hook: 94840, size 12-16.
Thread: Black 3/0 mono-cord.
Tail: Mixed brown and grizzly hackle
          fibers.
Body: Dubbed muskrat.
Wing: White divided calf tail (sparse).
Hackle: Mixed brown and grizzly
          hackle.

BLACK GNAT
Hook: 94840, size 12-16.
Thread: Black 3/0 mono-cord.
Tail: Black hackle fibers.
Body: Fine black chenille.
Wing: Gray duck wing quill.
Hackle: Black neck hackle.

BLACK GNAT TRUDE
Hook: 94840, size 8-14.
Thread: Black 3/0 mono-cord.
Tail: Black hackle fibers.
Body: Dubbed black synthetic fur.
          Body should have a good plump
          taper.
Wing: Natural black calf tail.
Hackle: Black.

BLACK JASSID
Hook: 94838, size 16-22.
Thread: Black 6/0 pre-waxed.
Tail: None.
Body: Black neck hackle tied palmer
          and clipped close to hook.
Wing: One jungle cock eye tied flat
          over the back.
Hackle: One oversize black neck hackle
          trimmed flat on top and bottom.
          Trimmed on sides to size —
          spinner style.
Note: Tie in wing after hackle.

BLONDE TRUDE
Hook: 94840, size 12-16.
Thread: White 3/0 mono-cord.
Tail: Cream hackle fibers.
Body: Cream spun fur.
Wing: Light elk body hair.
Hackle: Cream neck hackle.

BLUE DUN
Hook: 94840, size 12-14; 94838,
          size 16-18.
Thread: Black 3/0 mono-cord (6/0 pre-
          waxed for size 18).
Tail: Blue dun hackle fibers.
Body: Dubbed muskrat.
Wing: Gray duck wing quill.
Hackle: Blue dun neck hackle.

BLUE QUILL
Hook: 94840, size 12-14; 94838,
          size 16-18.
Thread: Black 3/0 mono-cord.
Tail: Blue dun hackle fibers.
Body: Stripped peacock quill.
Wing: Gray duck wing quill.
Hackle: Blue dun neck hackle.

BLUE UPRIGHT
Hook: 94840, size 12-20.
Thread: Gray.
Tail: Blue dun hackle fibers.
Body: Light peacock quill. Reverse
          wrap the body with fine silver
          wire.
Wing: Natural gray duck quill sections
          tied upright and divided.
Hackle: Blue dun.

BLUE WING OLIVE
Hook: 94838, size 12-16.
Thread: Brown.
Tail: Dyed light gray hackle fibers.
Body: Dubbed brown olive synthetic
          fur.
Wing: Dyed gray elk hair tied upright
          and divided.
Hackle: Dyed light gray tied Waterwalker
          style.

BOX CAR (See Coachman Trude)
Hook: 90240, size 6-10.
Thread: Black A mono-cord.
Tail: Red hackle fibers.
Body: Peacock herl.
Wing: White calf tail.
Hackle: Brown saddle hackle.

BROWN AND GRAY
Hook: 94840, size 10-20.
Thread: Tan 3/0 mono-cord.
Tail: Mixed brown and grizzly
          hackle fibers.
Body: Dubbed fitch (cream dubbing).
Wing: None.
Hackle: Mixed brown and grizzly neck
          hackle.

BYERLY'S PARACHUTE
Hook: 94840, size 10-14.
Thread: Yellow 3/0 mono-cord.
Tail: Deer body hair medium color.
Body: Underbody, orange yarn. Back,
          deer body hair humpy style.
Wing: Butts of tail/back hair posted
          into single wing and trimmed to
          length.
Hackle: Mixed brown and grizzly
          hackle.

CARSON KING

Hook:	94840, size 10-14.
Thread:	Black 3/0 mono-cord.
Tail:	Golden pheasant tippet.
Body:	Peacock herl.
Wing:	None.
Hackle:	Brown neck hackle.

CARSON QUEEN

Hook:	94840, size 10-14.
Thread:	Yellow 3/0 mono-cord.
Tail:	Golden pheasant tippet.
Body:	Yellow floss.
Wing:	None.
Hackle:	Brown neck hackle.

COMPARA-DUN

Hook:	94838, size 14-20.
Thread:	Cream (change color with fly color), 3/0 mono-cord (6/0, size 18-20).
Tail:	Cream hackle fibers tied split.
Body:	Cream dubbed poly; one turn goes ahead of the wing (tan, brown, olive or gray).
Wing:	Deer body hair erected only to 45 degrees.
Hackle:	None.

DARK CADDIS

Hook:	94840, size 8-14.
Thread:	Yellow 3/0 mono-cord.
Tail:	Yellow hackle fibers.
Body:	Yellow wool yarn.
Rib:	Yellow tied palmer over body.
Wing:	Dark deer body hair tied over the body and extending length of body only.

DARK CAHILL

Hook:	94840, size 12-14; 94838, size 16-18.
Thread:	Black 3/0 mono-cord.
Tail:	Brown hackle fibers.
Body:	Dubbed muskrat fur.
Wing:	Barred lemon woodduck tied upright and divided.
Hackle:	Brown.

DARK STONE (See Parks' Salmon Fly)

Hook:	38941, size 8.
Thread:	Black.
Tail:	None.
Body:	Tangerine orange synthetic yarn.
Rib:	Dark furnace hackle tied palmer over the body.
Wing:	Dyed coffee brown bucktail.
Hackle:	Dark furnace tied on as a collar in front of wing.

DAVE'S HOPPER

Hook:	9671, Size 6-14.
Thread:	Black.
Tail:	Natural tannish gray deer body hair dyed red.
Body:	Yellow yarn. After yarn is tied in, make a small loop with the yarn extending it half way over the tail.
Rib:	Brown hackle tied palmer over body.

Wing:	Under, yellow deer hair. Over, Brown mottled turkey wing quill sections tied tent style over body and covering underwing.
Head:	Spun deer body hair trimmed to shape. Leave a few natural tips extending out on both sides. Heads should be trimmed flat on top and bottom.

DEER HEAD HOPPER

Hook:	9672, size 2-10.
Thread:	Tan A mono-cord.
Tail:	None.
Body:	Tan chenille.
Rib:	Grizzly palmer.
Wing:	Deer body hair.
Hackle:	None.
Head:	Clipped deer hair muddler style.

DEERHOPPER

Hook:	9671, size 6-12.
Thread:	Black 3/0 mono-cord.
Tail:	Red hackle fibers.
Body:	Clipped yellow deer hair spun and clipped.
Rib:	Brown saddle hackle palmered and trimmed.
Wing:	Brown mottled turkey quill.
Hackle:	Brown and gray mix.

DELTA WING CADDIS

Hook:	94840, size 8-14.
Thread:	Olive 3/0 mono-cord.
Body:	Light olive fur (mink, etc.) or the proper shade dubbing to match the natural.
Wing:	Two gray hen hackle tips, or the color to match the natural.
Hackle:	Brown, or any quality dry fly hackle to match the legs of the natural.

DENNY'S SPECIAL

Hook:	9672 (3X long), size 6-10.
Thread:	Black 3/0 mono-cord.
Tail:	Light elk body hair.
Body:	Cream yarn.
Rib:	Tan thread.
Wing:	Light elk body hair.
Hackle:	Two brown hackles with fluorescent orange yarn tied between the two hackle segments in a narrow band.

DESCHUTES DEMON

Hook:	7948A, size 4.
Thread:	Black A mono-cord.
Tail:	Orange hackle fibers.
Body:	Yellow floss.
Rib:	Gold embossed tinsel.
Wing:	Under, coarse deer body hair. Over, sparse white bucktail.
Hackle:	Orange hackle (throat only).

DICK'S SOFA PILLOW

Hook:	9672 (3X long shank), size 4-8.
Thread:	Yellow A mono-cord.

Tail:	Coarse bucktail or deer body hair.
Body:	Yellow yarn.
Rib:	Brown hackle palmered then clipped.
Wing:	Red squirrel tail.
Hackle:	None.
Head:	Spun deer hair muddler style — very large.

DRY MUDDLER MINNOW

Hook:	9672, size 8-14.
Thread:	Yellow 3/0 mono-cord.
Tail:	Brown mottled turkey quill.
Body:	Yellow polypropolene yarn.
Wing:	Under, white calf tail. Over, two mottled brown turkey quills matched and tied curve up.
Head:	Clipped deer hair; trimmed flat under head.

ELK HAIR CADDIS

Hook:	94840, size 8-16.
Thread:	Tan.
Body:	Dubbed hare's ear fur.
Rib:	Gold wire.
Wing:	Tannish cream elk hair.
Hackle:	Furnace.

ENGLISH STONE

Hook:	94840, size 8-16.
Thread:	Black 3/0 mono-cord.
Tail:	Golden pheasant tip.
Body:	Yellow yarn (back one-third); blue dun gray (front two-thirds).
Wing:	Light turkey tied flat on both sides.
Hackle:	Light ginger.
Antennae:	Two horse hair fibers or moose mane.

FEMALE ADAMS

Hook:	94840, size 12-16.
Thread:	Black 3/0 mono-cord.
Tail:	Brown and grizzly neck hackle mixed.
Body:	Dubbed muskrat.
Tag:	One turn of fine yellow chenille.
Wing:	Grizzly hackle points.
Hackle:	Brown and grizzly neck hackle mixed.

F.F.F.

Hook:	94840, size 10-14; 94838, size 16-18.
Thread:	Black.
Tail:	Black and brown hackle fibers mixed.
Body:	Dubbed dark brown fur.
Wing:	Grizzly hackle tips tied upright and divided.
Hackle:	Black and brown mixed.

FLOAT'N FOOL

Hook:	94840, size 10-14.
Thread:	Black 3/0 mono-cord.
Tail:	White calf tail.
Body:	Peacock herl.
Wing:	White calf tail single post.
Hackle:	Mixed brown and grizzly tied parachute style.

FLOATING NYMPH
Hook: 94840, size 6-18; 94838, size 16-20.
Thread: Olive A 3/0 mono-cord.
Tail: Hackle fibers (dark brown, light brown or ginger, dark blue dun), split no-hackle dun style.
Body: Spun fur (dark reddish brown, light tan or amber, olive, medium brown) or Fly-Rite in No. 6, 30, 3 or 20.
Wing case: Fur (grayish black, dark gray Belgian mole, dark gray, yellow) or poly stacked; or goose quill segments tied in and pulled over stacked thorax.
Legs: Not required. (If desired, match with tails.)

FLUTTERING CADDIS
Hook: 94840, size 12-16.
Thread: Black 3/0 mono-cord.
Tail: None.
Body: Dubbed muskrat.
Wing: Dun hackle.
Hackle: Blue dun neck hackle.

FLYING CADDIS
Hook: 94840, size 8-12.
Thread: Brown.
Tail: Brown hackle fibers.
Body: Dubbed yellow synthetic fur. Brown hackle palmered over the body.
Wing: Natural gray duck quill sections tied upright and divided.
Hackle: Brown. This hackle is in addition to that palmered over the body.

GIANT STONE FLY
Hook: 9672 3X long, size 4-8.
Thread: Orange A mono-cord.
Tail: Two stiff gray duck wing quill fibers.
Body: Woven. Under is orange yarn, top is dark brown yarn.
Rib: Brown saddle hackle palmered.
Wing: Brown bucktail — as long as mid-length of tail.
Hackle: Brown saddle.
Antennae: Same material as tail.

GINGER QUILL
Hook: 94840, size 12-14; 94838, size 16-18.
Thread: Black 3/0 mono-cord (7/0 for 18's).
Tail: Light ginger hackle fibers.
Body: Stripped peacock quill.
Rib: Tan 3/0 mono-cord.
Wing: Natural light gray duck quill sections tied upright and divided.
Hackle: Light ginger.

GOLDEN STONE
Hook: 94840, size 8-16.
Thread: Yellow 3/0 mono-cord.
Body: Golden yellow yarn.
Rib: Light ginger hackle tied palmer style then clipped.

Wing: Light elk hair fibers tied bucktail style.
Hackle: Light ginger hackle.

GRAY HACKLE PEACOCK
Hook: 94840, size 12-16.
Thread: Black 3/0 mono-cord.
Tail: Red hackle fibers.
Body: Peacock herl.
Wing: None.
Hackle: Grizzly neck hackle.

GRAY HACKLE YELLOW
Hook: 94840, size 12-16.
Thread: Black 3/0 mono-cord.
Tail: Red hackle fibers.
Body: Yellow floss.
Rib: Gold mylar tinsel.
Wing: None.
Hackle: Grizzly neck hackle.

GRAY PARACHUTE
Hook: 94840, size 12-16.
Thread: Black 3/0 mono-cord.
Tail: Ginger hackle fibers.
Body: Dubbed muskrat.
Wing: White calf tail erect.
Hackle: Ginger neck hackle tied parachute style.

GRAY YELLOW NO HACKLE
Hook: 94838, size 14-20.
Thread: Tan 6/0 pre-waxed mono-cord.
Tails: Golden ginger hackle fibers tied split.
Body: Yellow fur or Fly-Rite No. 4.
Wing: Light gray duck shoulder feathers.
Hackle: None.

GREEN DRAKE PARACHUTE
Hook: 94840, size 8-14.
Thread: Black 3/0 mono-cord.
Tail: Dyed light olive deer hair tied paradrake style.
Body: A continuation of the tail.
Rib: Brown A mono-cord.
Wing: Dyed light olive deer hair.
Hackle: Green-dyed grizzly hackle tied parachute style.

GRIZZLY WULFF
Hook: 94840, size 10-14.
Thread: Black 3/0 mono-cord.
Tail: Brown bucktail.
Body: Yellow acetate floss hardshell.
Wing: Brown bucktail.
Hackle: Mixed brown and grizzly (brown may be saddle hackle).

GULPER SPECIAL
Hook: 94840, size 16.
Thread: Olive 3/0 mono-cord.
Tail: Moose body hair.
Body: Dubbed pale olive poly.
Wing: Gray poly yarn post.
Hackle: Grizzly hackle parachute style.

HAIR WING CADDIS
Hook: 94840, size 12-16.
Thread: Black 3/0 mono-cord.
Tail: None.

Body: Single barbules from turkey quill.
Wing: Dark elk body hair.
Hackle: Brown hackle.

HAIRWING NO HACKLE
Hook: 94838, size 14-20.
Thread: Gray 3/0 mono-cord.
Tail: Blue dun hackle fibers.
Body: Tightly dubbed muskrat.
Wing: Deer body hair fanned.
Hackle: None.

HAIRWING WESTERN MARCH BROWN
Hook: 94840, size 8-22.
Thread: Black.
Tail: Brown neck hackle fibers.
Body: Grayish brown dubbed rabbit fur.
Rib: One strand of gold floss.
Wing: Mottled brown turkey divided and tied upright or woodduck breast.
Hackle: Medium brown, blue dun, or fiery furnace.

HANK OF HAIR
Hook: 94838, size 12-18.
Thread: Black 3/0 mono-cord.
Tail: None.
Body: None.
Wing: Deer body hair, tied short.
Hackle: None.

HORNER'S DEER HAIR
Hook: 94840, size 10-16.
Thread: Black 3/0 mono-cord.
Tail: Deer body hair (dark tones).
Body: Deer body hair over thread under body (humpy style).
Wing: Deer body hair.
Hackle: Mixed brown and grizzly.

HUMPY HOPPER
Hook: 9671, sizes 6-14.
Thread: Tan mono-cord.
Tail: Golden pheasant.
Body: Yellow poly yarn.
Rib: Brown hackle clipped palmer.
Underwing: Yellow bucktail.
Overwing: Natural deer body hair tied reversed with wing over the eye and then pulled back humpy style and secured at the wing position.

JUGHEAD
Hook: 9672, size 4-8.
Thread: Black A mono-cord.
Tail: Natural medium elk hair.
Body: Orange yarn.
Rib: Brown hackle, clipped palmer.
Wing: Natural elk body hairs; overwing — red squirrel tail.
Hackle: None.
Head: Spun brown hair, trimmed.

LIGHT BUCKTAIL CADDIS
Hook: 94840, size 8-14.
Thread: White 3/0 mono-cord.
Tail: Cream hackle fibers.
Body: Cream (pale yellow) yarn.
Wing: Light elk hair.
Hackle: Cream saddle hackle palmered.

LIGHT CADDIS
Hook: 94840, size 10-16.
Thread: Black 3/0 mono-cord.
Tail: Light elk hair.
Body: Light cream dubbing.
Rib: Ginger hackle tied palmer style.
Wing: Slate gray duck quills.
Hackle: Very pale light blue dun.

LITTLE MARYAT
Hook: 94840, size 12-18.
Thread: Black 3/0 mono-cord.
Tail: Cream hackle fibers.
Body: Narrow strand of natural raffia.
Wing: Gray duck wing quill.
Hackle: Cream neck hackle.

MASON SMALL DRAKE
Hook: 94840, size 12.
Thread: Olive 3/0 mono-cord.
Tail: Two lengths of 3X mono-filament.
Body: Light gray muskrat.
Wing: Blue dun dyed calf tail.
Hackle: Blue dun tied parachute style.

McGINTY
Hook: 94840, size 8-16.
Thread: Black 3/0 mono-cord.
Tail: Red neck hackle fibers.
Body: One black and one yellow chenille wrapped to give striped effect. Use very fine chenille.
Wing: Irridescent blue quill feather found on mallard duck wing.
Hackle: Medium brown neck hackle.

MINK TAIL CADDIS
Hook: 94840, size 10-18.
Thread: Black 3/0 mono-cord.
Tail: None.
Rib: None.
Body: Peacock herl, partially stripped.
Wing: Mink tail hair tied down.
Hackle: Mixed brown and grizzly.

MONKEY WING CADDIS
Hook: 94840, size 10-14.
Thread: Black 3/0 mono-cord.
Tail: None.
Body: Brown/olive dubbing (Fly-Rite No. 32).
Wing: Silver barred monkey hair.
Hackle: Mixed brown and grizzly dressed heavily. (Brown saddle hackle recommended or two brown neck hackles.)

MONTANA BUCKTAIL
Hook: 9671, size 6-10.
Thread: Tan.
Tail: Golden pheasant tippet fibers.
Body: Orange floss.
Wing: Light tan elk hair tied over body and extending to the end of body.
Hackle: Grizzly tied palmer over body.

MUDDLED HOPPER
Hook: 9671 2X long, size 6-14.
Thread: Black A mono-cord.

Tail: Red hackle fibers.
Body: Yellow yarn.
Rib: Brown hackle palmered — one size smaller than normal.
Wing: Mottled turkey wing quill.
Hackle: Single bank of spun natural deer hair with tips done muddler style.
Head: Died yellow spun deer hair clipped muddler style.

NORM WOODS SPECIAL
Hook: 9671, size 6.
Thread: Black A mono-cord.
Tail: Red squirrel tail.
Body: Orange yarn with rib of brown palmered hackle clipped to equal hook gap.
Wing: Brown bucktail.
Hackle: Single brown hackle wound palmer style over orange yarn base.

PARACHUTE ADAMS
Hook: 94840, size 10-14.
Thread: Black 3/0 mono-cord.
Tail: Mixed brown and grizzly hackle fibers.
Body: Dubbed muskrat.
Wing: White calf tail, single post.
Hackle: Mixed brown and grizzly tied parachute style.

PHEASANT CADDIS
Hook: 94840, size 10-14.
Thread: Olive 3/0 mono-cord.
Tail: None.
Body: Dark green yarn.
Rib: Brown palmered hackle clipped close to the body.
Wing: Small brown pheasant body feather lacquered and rolled.
Hackle: Brown neck hackle.

PHEASANT HOPPER
Hook: 9671, size 6-14.
Thread: White A mono-cord.
Tail: Peccary.
Body: Yellow poly yarn.
Rib: Furnace saddle tied palmer and trimmed.
Wing: Under, dyed yellow deer hair (sparse). Over, heavily lacquered pheasant body feather rolled over and trimmed.
Hackle: Sparsely spun unclipped deer hair.
Head: Clipped spun deer hair tied muddler style.

RED QUILL
Hook: 94840, size 10-14.
Thread: Brown 3/0 mono-cord.
Tail: Brown neck hackle fibers.
Body: Stripped peacock quill.
Wing: Medium gray duck quill.
Hackle: Reddish-brown neck hackle.

RIO GRANDE KING (Also called O'CONNOR TRUDE or RIO GRANDE KING)
Hook: 94840, size 10-16.
Thread: Black 3/0 mono-cord.
Tail: Golden pheasant tippets.

Body: Fine black chenille.
Wing: White calf tail (Trude style).
Hackle: Brown neck hackle.

ROYAL COACHMAN
Hook: 94840, size 12-16.
Thread: Black 3/0 mono-cord.
Tail: Golden pheasant tippet.
Tag: Red floss.
Body: Peacock (center segment red floss).
Wing: White duck wing quill.
Hackle: Coachman brown neck hackle.

ROYAL COACHMAN BUCKTAIL
Hook: 94840, size 8-16.
Thread: Black 3/0 mono-cord.
Tail: Golden pheasant tippet.
Body: Peacock herl, red floss center band.
Wing: White calf tail.
Hackle: Brown neck hackle.

SIERRA BRIGHT DOT
Hook: 94840, size 12-18.
Thread: Black 3/0 mono-cord.
Tail: Golden pheasant tippet.
Body: Fluorescent red floss.
Wing: None.
Hackle: Fore and aft, grizzly hackle for both.

SLATE WING OLIVE PARADUN
Hook: 94838, size 14-20.
Thread: Brown 6/0 pre-waxed.
Tail: Medium olive hackle fibers tied split.
Body: Medium olive fur ribbed with olive thread.
Wing: Dark slate poly parachute style.
Hackle: Medium olive parachute style.

SOFA PILLOW
Hook: 9671, size 4-8.
Thread: Black A mono-cord.
Tail: Red goose wing quill.
Body: Red floss.
Wing: Red squirrel tail.
Hackle: Brown saddle hackles.

SPENT MIDGE
Hook: 94838, size 16-22.
Thread: Black 6/0 mono-cord.
Tail: None.
Body: Stripped light colored hackle stem quill.
Wing: None.
Hackle: Very sparse grizzly tied parachute style.

SPENT WING ADAMS
Hook: 94840, size 12-14; 94838, size 16-18.
Thread: Black 3/0 mono-cord.
Tail: Brown and grizzly hackle fibers.
Body: Dubbed muskrat.
Wing: Grizzly hackle points (tied spent style - flat out from the sides of the hook).
Hackle: Brown and grizzly mixed.

SPRUCE
Hook: 94840, size 10-16.
Thread: Black 3/0 mono-cord.
Tail: Dark moose hair.
Body: Red floss, back half. Peacock herl, front half.
Wing: Badger hackle tips tied upright and divided.
Hackle: Badger saddles for large sizes; neck hackles for small sizes.

SPUN DEER HAIR HOPPER
Hook: 9671, size 6-14.
Thread: Tan A mono-cord.
Tail: Short trimmed red bucktail.
Body: Clipped light olive dyed deer hair.
Wing: Dark brown dyed deer hair.
Head: Clipped dark brown dyed deer hair.

STEPHENSON'S FLUTTERING STONE FLY
Hook: 94840, size 4-8.
Thread: Orange A mono-cord.
Tail: Orange poly yarn (knotted at the end to reduce fraying).
Wing: Deer body hair (long - tied in at tail position).
Body: Furnace, palmered, dressed very densely.
Hackle: Same as body.
Antennae: Two stripped brown hackle stems.

TRUCKEE RIVER SPECIAL
Hook: 94840, size 10-14.
Thread: Black 3/0 mono-cord.
Tail: None.
Body: Gray floss.
Wing: Rolled turkey wing quill trimmed to the caddis silhouette.
Hackle: Brown neck hackles.

WATERWALKER SERIES
Hook: 94840, size 10-14.
Thread: Brown; light yellow; gray; olive.
Tail: Moose hair.
Body: Dubbed synthetic fur — seal brown, cream, gray, or olive.
Wings: Brown elk hair tied upright and divided.
Hackle: Waterwalker style — brown, cream, grizzly, dyed olive.

WHITCRAFT
Hook: 94840, sizes 12-18.
Thread: Yellow 3/0 mono-cord.
Tail: Brown and grizzly hackle fibers mixed.
Body: Stripped peacock quill.
Rib: Tan mono-cord.
Wing: Grizzly hackle points.
Hackle: Brown and grizzly mixed.

WICKHAM'S FANCY
Hook: 94840, size 10-16.
Thread: Black 3/0 mono-cord.
Tail: Brown hackle fibers.
Body: Embossed gold tinsel.
Rib: Brown hackle tied over body palmer style.
Wing: Natural gray duck quill sections tied upright and divided.
Hackle: Brown.

WRIGHT'S ROYAL
Hook: 94840, size 10-14.
Thread: Black 3/0 mono-cord.
Tail: None.
Body: Aft segment, peacock herl. Fore segment, red floss.
Wing: Light elk body hair erected to 45 degrees.
Hackle: Brown neck wound sparse over peacock on the whole head.

VINCENT SEDGE
Hook: 94840, size 10-12.
Thread: Black 3/0 mono-cord.
Tail: Deer body hair.
Body: Green floss or poly yarn.
Wing: Deer hair underwing. Rolled turkey overwing.
Hackle: Brown neck hackle.

Fly Shops and Favored Patterns

ARIZONA

Don's Sport Shop, Inc.
Don Brooks
7803 E. McDowell Road
Scottsdale, Arizona 85257
1. Female Adams
2. Irresistible
3. Black Gnat
4. McGinty

The Hatch
Bob Rittenhouse
P.O. Box 5624
Tucson, Arizona 85705
1. Adams
2. Brown and Gray Mixed Hackle and Tail Cream Dubbed Body
3. Joe's Hopper (Deer hair head)
4. Ant (Black or cinnamon, dubbed body)
5. Black Gnat (Dubbed body)

CALIFORNIA

Alpine Bottle & Tackle
Doug Ford
P.O. Box 216
Markleeville, California 96120
1. Royal Coachman Bucktail
2. Carson King
3. Carson Queen
4. Renegade
5. Adams

Bucksport Sporting Goods
Greg Rice
3650 South Broadway
Eureka, California 95501
1. Black Ant
2. California Mosquito

Bud's Electric & Sporting Goods
H.L. Owens
P.O. Box 395

Truckee, California 95734
1. Ginger Quill
2. Wickham's Fancy
3. Gray Hackle Yellow
4. California Mosquito

Butch's Hunting & Fishing Center
Butch Olson
216 W. Main Street
Visalia, California 93277
1. Bird's Stone Fly
2. Adams
3. Humpy

Buz's Fly & Tackle Shop
Lance Wilkins
805 W. Tulare
Visalia, California 93277
1. Adams
2. Yellow Goofus Bug
3. Royal Wulff
4. Dave's Hopper
5. Monkey Wing Caddis
6. Light Bucktail Caddis

Creative Sports
2333 Boulevard Circle
Walnut Creek, California 94595
1. Yellow Humpy
2. Goddard Caddis
3. Light Cahill
4. Adams
5. Royal Wulff

Dale's Hackle & Tackle
Dale G. Lundquist
2634 W. Orangethorpe Avenue
Fullerton, California 92633
1. Royal Wulff (No. 10-16)
2. Hairwing Caddis (No. 14-16)
3. Blue Dun Humpy (No. 12-16)
4. Adams (No. 14-20)

Doug Kittredge's Sport Shop
James B. Butler
P.O. Box 598
Mammoth Lakes, California 93546
1. Male Adams
2. California Mosquito
3. King's River Caddis
4. Light Cahill
5. Black Gnat

Eddie Bauer, Inc.
Hal Rebholtz
120 Kearny Street
San Francisco, California 94101
1. Adams (No. 14-18)
2. Horner's Deer Hair (No. 14-16)
3. Mosquito (No. 14-18)
4. Gnat (No. 16-18)

Ernie's Tackle Shop
Michael A. Logue
P.O. Box 36
June Lake, California 93529
1. California Mosquito
2. Red Tail Mosquito
3. Black Gnat

Fall River Fly Shop
Bob Quigley
Star Route Glenburn
Fall River Mills, California 96028
1. Elk Hair Parachute
2. Olive Quill Spinner
3. Deer Hair Spider
4. Elk Hair Caddis
5. Adams
6. Light Cahill

Filson's Tackle & Sports
Jim Bartling
P.O. Box 962
Mammoth Lakes, California 93546
1. Ginger Quill (No. 16)
2. Light Cahill (No. 16)
3. Brown Sedge (No. 18)
4. Blue Upright (No. 20)
5. White/Black Spinner (No. 22)
6. Yellow Humpy (No. 14)

Fly Fishing Unlimited
William A. Kiene
2929 Fulton Avenue No. 3
Sacramento, California 95821

1. Humpy (Yellow, No. 6-18)
2. Royal Wulff (No. 8-14)
3. Adams (No. 14-18)
4. Light Cahill (No. 14-18)
5. Renegade (No. 8-14)

The Fly Shop
Brad Jackson and Mike Michalak
2727 Churn Creek Road
Redding, California 96001
1. Goddard Caddis (No. 10-18)
2. Deer Hair Spider (No. 14-18)
3. Poly Wing Spinner (Olive quill body, No. 14-18)
4. Adams (No. 12-18)
5. Muddled Salmon Fly

The Fly Hutch
Neil W. Bohannon
3423 El Camino Real
Santa Clara, California 95051
1. Olive Quill Paradun (No. 18)
2. Royal Wulff (No. 14)
3. Adams (No. 16)
4. Yellow Humpy (No. 14)

Hackle 'n Tackle Shop
Bob Foley
458 N. Humboldt Avenue
Willows, California 95988
1. Goofus Bug
2. Adams
3. Blue Dun
4. Mosquito

Hidden Rod Shop
John R. Hockenbrocht
2623 Gardenia Avenue
Signal Hill, California 90806
1. Hank of Hair
2. Humpy
3. Mosquito

Light's Fly Shop
Tom Light
4947 Folsom Boulevard
Sacramento, California 95816
1. Royal Wulff
2. Adams
3. Mosquito
4. Humpy
5. Light Cahill
6. Irresistible

The Millpond North
Kevin Muir
1601 Douglas Boulevard
Roseville, California 95678
1. Humpy (Red and yellow)
2. Adams
3. Black Ant
4. Royal Wulff
5. Mosquito

The Midge Fly Shop
2132 O'Toole Avenue
San Jose, California 95131
1. Humpy (Yellow body)

2. Adams
3. Blue Winged Olive
4. King's River Caddis
5. Irresistible Adams
6. Blue Dun

Ned Grey's Sierra Tackle
Ned Grey
P.O. Box 338
Montrose, California 91020
1. Sierra Bright Dot
2. Quill Gordon
3. Little Maryat
4. Adams

North Country Fly & Tackle
Lani Waller
150 Bellam No. 250
San Rafael, California 94902
1. Adams
2. King's River Caddis
3. Quill Gordon
4. Dark Cahill
5. Joe's Hopper
6. Humpy

Ojai Fisherman
Gerhard W. Orthuber
218 N. Encinal Avenue
Ojai, California 93023
1. California Mosquito (No. 16-18)
2. Adams (No. 14)
3. King's River Caddis (No. 12-16)
4. Gray Wulff (No. 10-12)
5. Goofus Bug (Black, No. 10-12)

Pat's Tackle Shop
Pat Pickett
P.O. Box 595
Bridgeport, California 93517
1. Female Adams
2. Ginger Quill
3. Black Gnat
4. Mosquito

Roos Atkins Sports Department
Fred Hasselgren
4th & Market Streets
San Francisco, California 94101
1. Buzz Hackle
2. Black Gnat Trude
3. Goofus Bug
4. Grizzly Wulff
5. Black Jassid

The San Francisco Fly Fisherman
Jim Chapman
530 Bush Street
San Francisco, California 94108
1. Yellow Humpy
2. Royal Wulff
3. Light Cahill
4. Joe's Hopper
5. Slate Wing Olive Paradun

Sport Center
Bob Stewart
325 Main Street
Salina, California 93901
1. Turkey Wing Caddis

Sportsmen's Den
John E. Kennedy
404 No. Mt. Shasta Boulevard
Mt. Shasta, California 96067
1. Gray Hackle Yellow (Silver ribbed)
2. Royal Coachman
3. Mosquito
4. Adams

Ted Fay
4154 Dunsmuir Avenue
Dunsmuir, California 96025
1. Adams (No. 12-14)
2. Gray Hackle Peacock (No. 12-14)
3. Humpy (Orange floss body)
4. Light Cahill (No. 14-16)
5. Joe's Hopper (No. 12 2X long, tan or yellow belly)

Tom's Liquor & Sporting
Thomas W. Polyniak
704 E. Alisal Street
Salinas, California 93901
1. Irresistible
2. Humpy

Turners
William C. Bancroft
607 E. Weber
Stockton, California 95201
1. Adams
2. Irresistible
3. California Mosquito
4. Royal Coachman

Western Sport Shop
Pat Pinckney
902 3rd Street
San Rafael, California 94901
1. Adams Irresistible
2. Humpy
3. Bucktail Caddis (Orange)
4. Light Cahill
5. Ginger Quill

COLORADO

Chuck Fothergill's Outdoor Sportsman
Chuck Fothergill
Box 88
Aspen, Colorado 81611
1. Yellow Goofus Bug
2. Royal Wulff
3. Adams
4. Irresistible
5. Red Quill

Creative Anglers
Kenn M. Ligas
2964 Peak Avenue
Boulder, Colorado 80302
1. Adams
2. Blue Wing Olive
3. Light Cahill
4. Trike Spinner
5. Spent Midge

The Fish 'n Hole
George Hamamoto
127 N. Tejon Street
Colorado Springs, Colorado 80903
1. Colorado King
2. Dave's Hopper
3. Adams
4. Blue Dun

The Flyfisher
Ken Walters
315 Columbine
Denver, Colorado 80206
1. Hairwing Western March Brown (No. 1)
2. Hairwing Rio Grande King (No. 12-14)

George M. Bodmer
4015 Valli Vista Road
Colorado Springs, Colorado 80909
1. Colorado King
2. Spruce Fly

Hank Roberts
1035 Walnut
Boulder, Colorado 80302
1. Irresistible
2. Deerhopper
3. Muddled Hopper
4. Giant Stone Fly
5. Rio Grande King Hairwing

Hank Roberts Sport Shop
Leon D. Sagaloff
122 W. Laurel Street
Ft. Collins, Colorado 80521
1. Adams
2. Henryville Special
3. Colorado King (Yellow body)
4. Fluttering Caddis (Blue dun)

The Ranch at Roaring Fork
Charles Loughridge
14913 Highway 82 — Ranch
Carbondale, Colorado 81623
1. Royal Wulff (No. 16-18)
2. Gray Parachute (No. 16)
3. Mosquito (No. 16-18)
4. Ginger Quill (No. 14-18)

Spring Creek
James D. Boyd
P.O. Box 1405
Ft. Collins, Colorado 80522
1. Adams
2. Adams Irresistible
3. Light Cahill
4. Delta Wing Caddis

Straightline Fly Shop
Frank E. Meek
703 Lincoln Avenue
Steamboat Springs, Colorado 80477
1. Ginger Quill (No. 16-20)
2. Quill Gordon (No. 16-20)
3. Goddard Caddis (No. 12-18)
4. Deer Hair Wing Caddis (No. 12-18)

IDAHO

Henry's Fork Anglers, Inc.
Mike Lawson
Box 487
St. Anthony, Idaho 83445
1. No Hackle (Duck quill wing)
2. Floating Nymph
3. Elk Hair Caddis
4. Henryville Special

Lakefork Flies
Don Hathaway
Highway 55, Route 1, Box 43
McCall, Idaho 83638
1. Royal Wulff
2. Adams
3. Mosquito
4. Humpy
5. Elk Hair Caddis

Snug
Bill Mason
Box 598
Sun Valley, Idaho 83353
1. Gray Yellow No Hackle
2. Adams (No. 16-20)
3. Royal Wulff (No. 12-16)
4. Mason Small Drake

Will Godfrey's Fly Fishing Center
P.O. Box 68
Island Park, Idaho 83429
1. Royal Wulff (No. 6-24)
2. Goofus Bug (No. 8-20)
3. Elk Hair Caddis (No. 10-18)
4. Adams (No. 10-24)
5. Yellow Buck Caddis (No. 10-12)

MONTANA

Angler's Agency
William R. Seeples
Deer Lodge, Montana
1. Adams
2. Humpy
3. Royal Wulff
4. Bucktail Caddis
5. Irresistible

Angler's Roost
Gene Snider
Route 1, Box 1209
Hamilton, Montana 59840
1. Royal Wulff
2. Adams
3. Hair Wing Variant
4. Quill Gordon

Bud Lilly Trout Shop
Bud Lilly
39 Madison Avenue
West Yellowstone, Montana 59758
1. Pheasant Hopper
2. Pheasant Caddis
3. Elk Hair Caddis
4. Green Drake Paradrake
5. Gulper Special

Bob Jacklin's Fly Shop
Bob Jacklin
Box 604
West Yellowstone, Montana 59758
1. Royal Wulff (No. 10-14)
2. Ginger Caddis (No. 14)
3. Gray Wulff (No. 12-14)
4. Blue Wing Olive (No. 16-18)

The Complete Fly Fisher
Philip N. Wright, Jr.
Box 105
Wise River, Montana 59762
1. Henryville Special
2. Spent Wing Adams
3. Wright's Royal
4. Stephenson's Fluttering Stone Fly
5. Gray Wulff

Dan Bailey's Fly Shop
Dan Bailey
Livingston, Montana 59047
1. Adams
2. Light Cahill
3. Quill Gordon
4. Royal Wulff
5. Grizzly Wulff

Four Rivers Sport Shop
Robert N. Palmer
205 S. Main
Twin Bridges, Montana 59754
1. Royal Wulff
2. Calico Irresistible
3. Humpy
4. King Caddis
5. Deer Head Hopper

Jim Danskin Tackle Shop
Jim Danskin
Box 276
West Yellowstone, Montana 59758
1. Royal Wulff
2. Adams
3. Goofus Bug (Yellow)
4. Goddard Caddis
5. King's River Caddis

Madison Sport Shop
James D. Kielley
Box 627
Ennis, Montana 59729
1. Royal Wulff
2. Yellow Bodied Humpy
3. Brown Trude
4. Dick's Sofa Pillow

Parks' Fly Shop
Richard C. Parks
Gardiner, Montana 59030
1. Coachman Trude
2. Royal Wulff
3. Parks' Salmon Fly
4. H & L Variant
5. Quill Gordon

Pat Barnes Tackle Shop
Pat Barnes
105 Yellowstone Avenue

West Yellowstone, Montana 59758
1. Adams
2. Goofus Bug
3. Jughead
4. Sofa Pillow

Ray's Tackle Shop & Guide Service
O. Raymond Champlin
P.O. Box 866
West Yellowstone, Montana 59758
1. House & Lot Variant
2. Jughead
3. Trude
4. Ginger Goofus (Yellow and red belly)
5. Adams

Streamside Anglers
Richard C. Anderson
1109 W. Broadway
Missoula, Montana 59801
1. Bucktail Caddis
2. Blonde Trude
3. Waterwalker Series
4. Goddard Caddis
5. Spun Deer Hair Hopper

NEBRASKA

Cabela's, Inc.
James W. Cabela
812 13th Avenue
Sidney, Nebraska 69162
1. Adams
2. Mosquito
3. Gray Hackle Peacock
4. Black Gnat
5. Royal Coachman

NEVADA

Mark Fore & Strike Sporting Goods
Butch Tureson
490 Kietzke Lane
Reno, Nevada 89504
1. Gray Hackle Yellow
2. Truckee River Special
3. Renegade
4. Humpy

NEW MEXICO

Charlie's Sporting Goods, Inc.
Charles Domenici
7401 H Menaul N.E.
Albuquerque, New Mexico 87110
1. Adams
2. Irresistible
3. Blue Quill
4. Renegade

OREGON

The Barbless Hook
Robert Patton

23 N. 23rd Place
Portland, Oregon 97210
1. Bucktail Caddis
2. Parachute Adams
3. Float-N-Fool
4. Byerly's Parachute
5. Denny's Special

The Caddis Fly Angling Shop
Bob Guard
688 Olive Street
Eugene, Oregon 97401
1. Yellow Elk Hair Caddis
2. Dry Muddler Minnow
3. Adams
4. Bird's Stone Fly
5. Hairwing No Hackle

Cascade Tackle Co.
Jerry & Del Applegarth
2425 Diamond Lake Boulevard
Roseburg, Oregon 97470
1. Royal Wulff
2. Irresistible
3. Yellow Humpy
4. Caddis Bucktail
5. Joe's Hopper

Don's Tackle Shop
Lola M. McClain
7622 S.E. Foster Rd.
Portland, Oregon 97206
1. Blue Upright
2. Adams Parachute
3. Norm Woods Special
4. English Stone
5. Deschutes Demon

Fur, Hook & Hackle
Robert Pierce
828 S. Central
Medford, Oregon 97501
1. Royal Coachman
2. Renegade
3. Dark and Light Caddis
4. Dark Stone (Polly Roseborough)
5. Golden Stone (Polly Roseborough)
6. Joe's Hopper

Kaufmann's Streamborn Fly Shop
Randall Kaufmann
P.O. Box 23032
Portland, Oregon 97233
1. Humpy (No. 10-24)
2. Parachute (No. 12-20)
3. Spinners (No. 12-26)
4. Elk Hair Caddis (No. 14-26)

Lamplight Trout Flies
Tony P. Hill
P.O. Box 196
Alsea, Oregon 97324
1. Elk Hair Caddis (Troth)
2. Adams/Adams Irresistible
3. Light Cahill/Light Irresistible
4. Hopper (Muddled or Letort)
5. Royal Wulff

Price's Angler's Corner
Al Price
15637 Sherrie Way
La Pine, Oregon 97739
1. Compara-Dun
2. Green Drake
3. Quill Gordon
4. Adams
5. Humpy

Stewart Custom Tackle
Douglas E. Stewart
17304 N.E. Halsey
Portland, Oregon 97230
1. Adams
2. Buck Coachman (Dry)
3. Buck Caddis (Orange)
4. English Stone
5. Gray Hackle Peacock

Wigwam Outdoor Stores
Bob Rinker
10209 N.E. Sandy Boulevard
Portland, Oregon 97220
1. Black Gnat
2. Blue Upright
3. Royal Coachman
4. Mosquito
5. Adams

Wigwam Outdoor Store
David L. Bevers
209 Tigard Plaza
Tigard, Oregon 97223
1. Renegade
2. Flying Caddis (Yellow)
3. Spruce
4. Gray Hackle Peacock
5. Royal Coachman

UTAH

Angler's Inn
Gean Snow
2265 Highland Drive
Salt Lake City, Utah 84106
1. Royal Wulff
2. Adams Calf Tail Wing
3. Light Cahill
4. Compara Dun
5. Mink Tail Caddis
6. Renegade

The Fly Line, Inc.
Bruce J. Barker
2935 Washington Boulevard
Odgen, Utah 84401
1. Elk Hair Caddis
2. Adams
3. Renegade (standard and reverse)
4. Light Cahill

Wolfes Sportsman's Headquarters
Bill Hayes
250 So. State
Salt Lake City, Utah 84111
1. Elk Caddis (Light)

2. King's River Caddis
3. Adams
4. Royal Wulff

WASHINGTON

Compleat Archer & Angler
Tom Darling
11714 15th N.E.
Seattle, Washington 98125
1. Vincent Sedge
2. Montana Bucktail
3. Tom Thumb
4. Box Car

Eddie Bauer, Inc.
E. Earl Younglove
1926 Third Avenue
Seattle, Washington 98101
1. Goofus Bug
2. Royal Coachman Bucktail
3. Grizzly Wulff
4. Bucktail Caddis
5. Adams

H & H Sportings Goods Co.
Gene Howell
814 Dupont
Bellingham, Washington 98225
1. Adams
2. Adams Irresistible
3. Royal Wulff
4. Light Cahill
5. Mosquito

Monson's Custom Tackle
Robert M. Monson
P.O. Box 518
Ephrata, Washington 98823
1. Adams
2. Mosquito
3. Royal Wulff
4. Renegade
5. Joe's Hopper

Neal's Fly & Tackle
Neal Daniel
5427 Pacific Avenue
Tacoma, Washington 98408
1. Caddis Buck
2. Adams

Patrick's Fly Shop
Jack Hutchinson
2237 Eastlake Avenue E
Seattle, Washington 98102
1. Adams
2. Montana Bucktail
3. Humpy
4. Various Wulffs

The Sport Cove, Inc.
Hardy Kruse
E. 6630 Sprague
Spokane, Washington 99206
1. F.F.F.
2. Adams

3. Royal Coachman
4. Black Ant
5. Renegade

WYOMING

Compleat Angler
Pete Test
Box 1337
Cody, Wyoming 82414
1. House & Lot (Peacock herl body, No. 10-12)
2. Adams (No. 14)
3. Goofus Bug (Yellow, No. 8)
4. Light Cahill (No. 14-16)
5. Royal Wulff (No. 14-16)
6. Gray Hackle Peacock (No. 10-12)

Garrett's Outdoor Shop
Robbie Garrett
332 W. Pine
Pinedale, Wyoming 82941
1. Joe's Hopper
2. Royal Wulff
3. Humpy

High Country Flies
Jay C. Buchner
Box 1022
Jackson, Wyoming 83001
1. Yellow Humpy
2. Royal Wulff
3. Joe's Hopper
4. Adams Irresistible
5. Adams; Green Humpy; Royal Coachman Trude; Light Cahill

Wyoming Waters Fly Shop
Ross Aune
1588 Sheridan Avenue
Cody, Wyoming 82414
1. Elk Hair Caddis
2. Red Quill
3. Whitcraft
4. Humpy Hopper
5. Gray Wulff

Trout Fishing Without Killing

I F the visitor to Yellowstone National Park were told that he could kill two chipmunks a day, five field mice, six ravens and one coyote, I predict the park visitor would be enraged. However, few visitors get upset with the park regulation that allows for the killing of trout in most of the park's waters. A sensitivity about preserving most mammals has spread faster than a sensitivity about preserving trout. To paraphrase Charles Brooks, "If trout could scream, fewer would be killed."

I have seen countless fishermen, primarily bait and spin, kill their catch and then later throw them away before ever reaching the dinner table. These fishermen never take the time to realize that they are killing a sophisticated living organism, a creature that has a right to live and an animal that in most places in the world is in short supply.

If I had my way I would make most streams and rivers catch-and-release fishing. As Chairman of the California Senate Select Committee on Fish and Game Wildlife, I am working to have certain streams in California designated as catch-and-release fishing only. Many fishermen, again primarily bait and spin, object to this approach saying, "What's the use of fishing if we can't keep our fish." Almost as if they were fishing as a means of providing meat rather than recreation. Many of these individuals would soon change their thinking if they calculated how much per pound each fish actually costs them. By the time the cost of gasoline, wear and tear on the automobile, motels, meals away from home and tackle are figured in, I venture to say that most trout caught are more expensive per pound than filet mignon. Therefore, those fishermen who fish for meat should stay home and not fish, buy steak, which I think tastes better, and save money. Trout fishing should never be looked upon as a means to acquire meat, but rather for enjoyment, relaxation and for a communion and agreement with nature. Fishing, for me, is more fun when there is not killing involved. In fact, a conscious effort to preserve the life of the fish brings a certain element of satisfaction to angling that a conscious effort to kill could never bring. The following procedures will ensure that a released fish has the best chance for survival.

1. Before starting to fish, pinch down your hook barb. This will result in few, if any, lost fish and will dramatically reduce the amount of tissue tearing and damage done to a hooked fish. Further, flies last longer this way as they are less often severely mangled in the process of removing them from the mouth of the fish.

2. Bring fish in as rapidly as possible. Fish under stress manufacture lactic acid, which their bodies have a difficult time eliminating. The longer a trout is played the more lactic acid is built up. Many trout are played to exhaustion and then released. Even though they appear to be healthy when they swim away, later they may die of lactic acid poisoning. The use of a net is helpful in shortening the time that a trout is played. I have found that I can land a big trout (over 15 inches) about one-third faster when I use a net.

3. A fish out of water is like a human under water — neither can breathe. Keep fish in the water as much as possible during the unhooking process. Remove the hook gently — if the barb is pinched down this process will be quick and easy. Further, do not squeeze the fish or handle it around the gills.

4. If the fish is hooked deeply, clip the leader as close as possible to the eye of the hook and then release the fish. The fish's body enzymes will make short work of your fly. I would much rather lose a dollar fly than to kill something as precious as a trout.

5. Make sure that a trout has maintained its equilibrium before it is released. This is especially important if the trout has been played extensively before it is released. Hold the fish gently facing upstream and slowly move the fish back and forth in order to force water, and thereby oxygen,

through the gills. Continue the back and forth movement until the fish is strong enough to squirm out of your gentle grasp.

6. Always release fish in slow water. Weakened fish released in fast water are often killed by the force of the current throwing them up against stream rocks.

7. If you wish to photograph large trout, lay the fish out on a soft bank or grass. A fish flopping around on a rocky area can do serious damage to itself. Never hold the fish up to be photographed by placing your fingers underneath its gill plates. This will do serious damage to its gills. Finally, have the camera setting ready before you lift the fish out of water. In this way you will minimize the amount of time the fish will have to go without oxygen.

Catch-and-release fishing will take hold nationally only if fly fishermen begin to pressure their State Fish and Game Commissioners and elected officials, primarily State Legislators, to actively sponsor and support designating certain waters as catch-and-release fishing. By writing your elected officials and State Fish and Game Commissioners and letting your feelings be known, it may make it possible for future generations of Americans to catch a native trout rather than a colorless planted trout which costs more to raise per pound than steak.

Selected Bibliography

THE following works have been helpful to the authors and we feel they should be included in every serious fly fisherman's library.

Bergman, Ray. *Trout.* New York: Knopf, 1938.

Blades, William F. *Fishing Flies and Fly Tying.* Pennsylvania: Stackpole and Heck, Inc., 1951.

Caucci, Al and Nastasi, Bob. *Hatches.* New York: Comparahatch, Ltd., 1975.

Dennis, Jack H., Jr. *Western Trout Fly Tying Manual.* Utah: Sun Lithographing Company, 1974.

DuBois, Donald. *The Fisherman's Handbook of Trout Flies.* New York: A. S. Barnes, 1960.

Edsen, Leonard J. *Flies.* New York: Barnes, 1950.

Hellekson, Terry. *Popular Fly Patterns.* Utah: Peregrine Smith, Inc.

Hinsdill, Harold. *Fly Patterns and Their Origins.* Michigan: Westshore Publications, 1943.

LaFontaine, Gary. *The Challenge of the Trout.* Montana: The Mountain Press, 1976.

Leiser, Eric. *Fly Tying Materials.* New York: Crown Publishers, Inc., 1973.

Marbury, Mary Orvis. *Favorite Flies and Their History.* Massachusetts: Branford Company, reprint 1955.

Marinaro, Vincent. *A Modern Dry Fly Code.* New York: Putnam, 1950; Crown, 1970.

Schwiebert, Ernest. *Nymphs.* New York: Winchester Press, 1972.

Swisher, Doug and Richards, Carl. *Fly Fishing Strategy.* New York: Crown Publishers, Inc., 1975.

- - - - - *Selective Trout.* New York: Crown Publishers, Inc., 1971.

Wright, Leonard. *Fishing the Dry Fly as a Living Insect.* New York: E. P. Dutton, 1972.